Uplifting THE PAIN
— BY —
FOSTERING GROWTH MINDSET THROUGH POETRY NOW

Middle School
Teacher's Manual

GAIL CARTER-CADE

DEDICATION

To my mother, Merylene Carter, who has consistently supported me in all my undertakings and stood by my side. She insisted that I should publish this book as soon as possible since it might be useful to someone. Regretfully, Ike and Merylene Carter, my devoted parents, passed away before this book was released. They will always be cherished, greatly loved, and missed.

Dedicating this book to my daughters, The G girls: Gala, Gasia, Gazenea, and my grandson Galante, gives me great joy. My motivation for writing about behavioral and learning styles is to maybe assist others who may be facing comparable difficulties. I appreciate and deeply love you for your bravery in facing the challenges you faced.

Special Thanks:

Husband: Ezekiel Cade
Educators: Mrs. E. Rene' Dupre, Mrs. Amber Brown

Uplifting the Pain
by Fostering Growth Mindset Through Poetry
Teachers Manual
Copyright © 2024 by Gail Carter-Cade
Publisher: GA LA CAR
gailcarter-cade@upliftingthepain.com
www.upliftingthepain.com
Publishing consultant:
ISBN: 979-8-9864272-6-3

All rights reserved. No part of this publication may be reproduced, duplicated, transmitted, stored in a retrieval system, noncommercial or commercialized in whole, or in part, in any form or by any means, including photographing, photocopying, recording, or other electronic or mechanical methods, without the prior written permission of the publisher, except in the care of brief questions embodied in critical reviews and certain other noncommercial uses permitted by copyright law. For permission requests, write to the publisher, addressed: Attention Publisher: Preproduction Permission.
Publisher: Gail Carter-Cade
   www.upliftingthepain.com

Disclaimer

The information and references shared in this text in the hopes the reader will gain more insight into their children, students, or any adults dealing with different behavioral and learning styles. This book is not a substitute for the medical or mental health advice of physicians. This information does not prescribe any treatment but rather suggests seeking help or information to benefit your circumstances. The reader should regularly consult a physician, psychiatrist, psychologist, counselor, or teacher in matters relating to his/her health or mental health and particularly with respect to any symptoms may require a diagnosis, medical attention, or suggestions. Seek a professional consultation before altering your current medical or mental health treatment plan. It does not offer a diagnosis, professional counseling, or medical treatment. This is an effort to offer practical, useful information from experiences with which you may identify. Each experience may vary, and you need to seek professional guidance. Students aged 5 - 17 should be supervised when reading or viewing the literature within these pages. The readings may not be suitable for children to view or read unsupervised because of the content. The author is not liable or held responsible for any alleged damages caused indirectly or directly by the information cited in this book. Everything presented in this book is an opinion. We do not endorse the websites referenced. Please be advised. All materials contained in this book are suggested at the reader's discretion.

Table of Contents

Introduction	5
I Didn't Do Nothing	14
First Day	15
So Fast, So Fast	16
Discern	17
Hard	18
Expression	19
Twitch	20
I Can't Help	21
My Child	22
Get Him Back	23
The Way, I See It	24
I scream, I fight, I'm mad	25
My Father Figure	26
Clean	27
Focus	28
Hunger	29
Sway	30
I Don't Trust	31
Stutter	32
Here, There and Everywhere	33
Explode	34
Expectation	35
Don't Touch	36
You Yell	37
Never Wrong	38
Slow	40
My Hair	41
Sound	42
Size Me	43
Just Read	44
She Thinks She's Cute	45
My Mom	46

Down Hearted	47
Out My Name	48
Clumsy	49
Bully	50
Math	51
Answers Right	52
Why I Don't Try	53
A Loss	54
Leave Me Alone	55
Shaking	56
Contrary	57
Hurt	59
Process	60
Deaf	61
What's Wrong with Me?	62
Comprehend	63
Wheelchair	64
Wheelchair	64
Not a Quarter	65
Get It Right	66
Smart	67
Looking Bleak	68
You've Changed My World	69
I Don't Care	70
To Write Right	71
Special Education	72
Take Care of Me	73
No Excuse	74
I Didn't Mean To	75
I Can't Get to School	76
I Got it All	77
Yes, I Can	78
Yes, I Am	79

Introduction

WELCOME

This book is presented in a considerate and compassionate manner, with the hope that it would be appreciated as a useful resource for gaining a deeper understanding of the distinctive behavioral and learning approach. Meeting the needs of students and staff members in a timely manner will help them become successful and productive. Students will benefit from this realistic interactive poetry workbook, which provides them with mind-altering and empathic experiences that will improve their connections with teachers and other students both inside and outside of the classroom. It also sheds light on the roots of behavioral and learning processes and offers a deeper understanding.

About The Author

GAIL CARTER-CADE: Gail Carter-Cade is an esteemed educator and author dedicated to promoting empathy and understanding in the classroom. With a background in education and a passion for poetry, she aims to revolutionize teaching mindset practices and improve educational outcomes for all students.

Amber Brown, a Duval County School Teacher, attests to the transformative power of Carter-Cade's work, stating, "Insightful...thought provoking conversations that opened my eyes to a lot of different perspectives" and "you must connect before you correct". Brown's endorsement underscores this resourceful book's ability to foster empathy and understanding among educators, paving the way for more meaningful teacher-student relationships.

Mission:

To provide realistic interactive workbooks that show the underlying causes of behavioral and academic difficulties and promote growth mindset solutions that are uplifting and embracing to help students overcome their obstacles and find several paths to achievement.

Outline:

Students can be mysterious to many teachers, and if they don't behave as expected, they might be seen as misbehaving. Frequently, these actions are dismissed or put in custody. Regretfully, there aren't many resources available to educators that address the issues and underlying causes of behavior issues and learning difficulties. Teachers now must deal with an ever-growing range of challenges and expectations both within and outside of the classroom. They will frequently feel discouraged and isolated in their endeavors as a result.

Gaining insight helps improve tolerance and understanding so that teachers can respond to students in the most suitable way. Relationships between students and teachers are frequently found in miscommunication. This resource, "Uplifting The Pain by Fostering Growth Mindset Through Poetry Now" offers insight into student's behavior and learning preferences to enhance academic and social-emotional results. It has more than 200 poems that can be beneficial for instructors, parents, and students to work together.

It is perfect for organizations who work with students directly now and for those that train students to become career-oriented educators. The teacher-student and student-student connections in the classroom may be enhanced by the poems. Teachers will find it simpler to be more at ease, adapt, and change to meet the needs of the student as a result. When they need emotional or academic support, students will then feel at ease approaching a teacher or another student to voice their wants and opinions without disruption in the classroom.

Fostering Growth Mindset Through Poetry

Using poetry to cultivate a growth mindset is a strategy that incorporates understanding, compassion, sensitivity, and insight to help us learn from our experiences and those of others. expanding knowledge of what students go through at home and at school. Through the eyes of the students, the enthralling rhythmic poetry reveals and soothes the underlying causes of the traumatic facts and experiences, enabling individuals to see pass their challenges and adversities and use them as opportunities for constructive growth, while also turning unfavorable circumstances into positive ones. By practicing mindfulness, students learn to acknowledge the difficult experiences of their and peers without downplaying or exaggerating their own feelings. Converting negativity into positivity, compassion into empathy, and the development of a sense of community connection.

Teacher's Manual:

Enhancing student outcomes and teacher practice are the two main objectives of the framework's manual introduction. Teachers can concentrate on teaching new materials by using their teacher's manual and carry out inclusive education-promoting activities with the use of their teachers' manual. The purpose of this teaching manual is to spread new knowledge. The manual provides school leaders and teachers with a collection of poetic activities that can be directly implemented. Teaching practices are modeled and broken down into component parts to be fully understood.

Most poems' topic selections promote original thought, investigation, and analysis—all crucial components of the educational process. We want to engage in active, hands-on learning with students as they investigate poetry themes. It is our belief that true comprehension and admiration of poetry, as well as the delight of education, can only raise your student's complete participation in it.

Regarding workload, take notice that this workbook has a wide range of poetry to provide students with multiple ways to interact with the content. It is not required of students to finish every assignment. Depending on the areas in which the student needs to improve, you can decide which poems to concentrate on each week. You may also allow students to turn in written tasks partially orally. As your student advances, keep a watch on their workload and make necessary adjustments to allow them to prioritize meaningful learning experiences.

It is preferable not to provide your student with access to this guidebook for obvious reasons. It is important to support each student in developing their own solutions, and occasionally a student may go above and beyond what is asked of them in the assignment. We should support this! As soon as a student provides an incorrect response to a factual question, you may correct them. The learning process should always take precedence over feelings of judgment. If a student consistently provides erroneous answers on a given topic, it indicates that there are areas they should review. If a student's responses are the same as those in the teacher's manual, you should warn them about plagiarism and stress the value of producing original work. Many students understand this concept and its ramifications,

Goal:

To transform empathy into compassion and a possible negative into a positive, we need to cultivate feelings of connection and caring. It's critical to provide students with appropriate guidance as they express their suffering in their own terms. Knowledge that has been gained should be highlighted. The last point should emphasize the fresh perspective or development in thought as well as potential applications. All students are expected to make progress in these areas.

Student Achievement Objectives:

The goal of the student achievement objective is to exhibit higher order thinking abilities to others. Their actions serve as evidence that they have learned. A student needs to adopt a new mindset to provide an accurate response.

1. To empower kids to and share feelings through written expression and orally
2. To build empathy among peers and adults
3. To build classroom community and trust
4. To learn resilience and grit
5. To build hope and coping strategies

Application Growth Targets

1. Acquiring a growth-oriented mindset
2. Strengthens students resolve to take charge of their own life
3. Students consistently exercise self-discipline and self-control
4. Students associate with like-minded individuals
5. Students gain a deeper comprehension of who they are via self-awareness

Assessment

To foster understanding and learning we look for evidence of their understanding. We search for proof of their comprehension to promote learning and understanding. We search for evidence of a newly acquired understanding when evaluating student learning. Through observing them, having talks with them, conversing with them, reading their work, and listening to them. During guided and cooperative practice, we evaluate by facilitating discussions, paying attention to what the students have to say, and engaging in dialogue with them.

We discuss with them and thoroughly review their written responses to evaluate their individual work. We can keep an eye on their comprehension throughout the whole-class sharing session when they talk about what they have learned and share their fresh viewpoints with one another.

Specifically, the problem, previous point of view and the new outlook. This type of continuous assessment not only indicates what students can do, but it also helps us determine how successful our previous education was and what more we need.

Teachers can use role play to assess student's understanding or perspective on the role of the characters, or their engagement and involvement during the role play.

Presentation Outline Guide

- **Introduction**

1. Introduce the setting and characters
2. Explain the relationship between the characters
3. Introduce the topic being discussed
4. Role-Play Skit
5. Conclusion

- **Conclusion Sentence**—End the presentation strongly

Review: Identifies the root of the pain, previous point of view and the new outlook.

Materials:

"Uplifting The Pain of Behavioral and Learning Styles by Fostering Growth Mindset Through Poetry Now" Workbook and Teacher's Manual.

Instructional Strategies:

Instructional methods are those that will be applied repeatedly to make sure students meet the learning objective. Strategies like modeling, progressive release, remediation and extension in small groups, data chats, formative feedback, etc. are a few examples. Each example ought to provide an explanation of the elements of that tactic. Creating rules for appropriate behavior in a collective setting.

1. Self-reflection, which helps students have a better opinion of "knowing themselves"
2. Using new mindset ideas to guide decision-making in their daily lives
3. Forming a connection with their peers through shared ideologies
4. Some of the poem's key and supporting details have been underlined for you

Additional Questions:

Students benefit from more questions that define values in the following manners.

◇	**Additional Questions:** Students benefit from more questions that define values in the following manners.
1	**Literal questions:** These fundamental "who, what, when, where, and why" inquiries gauge knowledge of facts. They should not be the only focus, even if they are necessary for laying the groundwork.
2	**Inferential questions:** Students are encouraged to think beyond the text by using inferential questions to make connections, infer meaning, and form conclusions. "From the student's actions, what can you deduce about their emotional state?" or "How does this incident relate to another section of the narrative?" are some instances.
3	**Evaluative questions:** Questions that need evaluation: These push students to think critically, assess, and make judgments. Do you believe the character chose the right course of action? What makes sense or what doesn't? or "How successfully did the author convey the setting through imagery?" are a few examples

Schedule Guide

Scheduled Time: 25-30 minutes This activity will take an estimated total of twenty-five to thirty minutes

Teacher's Guide:

All groups need guidance

Set clear expectations

Student can opt out of the classroom discussion (If student is uncomfortable)

Teacher reads poem title aloud

Teacher asks for a show of hands of those who are familiar with the topic of the poem

Teacher walks around paying particular attention to how the poem is affecting the students

The teacher moves around the room actively listening in to conversations

Listening to how the students are paraphrasing the poems

Redirect at teachers' discretion

Modeling:

Teacher modeling is a strategy that helps students learn by demonstrating concepts, processes, skills, or behaviors. Here are some examples of teacher modeling:

> ***First Day: Read this poem: "I Didn't Do Nothing"**
>
> The goal of the first day of school is to promote mindset growth from the beginning. The poem will introduce and remind students of the purpose and importance of school rules. Students can use the note page provided in the workbook.

Step 1. Independent Reading/Poem Study: (Scheduled Time: 8 -10 minutes)

Student Instruction:

a) Silently read poem closely

b) Students may privately express their feelings about the poem

c) Review title and illustrations

d) Skimming and scanning main points

e) Annotate and take notes, highlight, underline, or circle key parts of poem

f) Activate prior knowledge and experiences

g) Answer questions

h) Identify main character (draw a circle) and describe character using key details(underline)

i) Identify points of the poem that gave student insight

j) Identify the challenge(pain)

k) Identify mindset growth

l) Identify useful information to share in your school community

m) Note if student personally identifies with the poem (put a check next to title)

Step 2. Turn and talk: Use as time permits (Scheduled Time: 8 -10 minutes)

Student Instruction:

The turn-and-talk routine:

Modeling the turn-and-talk routine should be the first step in teaching students how it looks and sounds

As part of an instructional process, students converse briefly with a peer while applying their material knowledge. The poetry is given to the class to discuss. Students turn to face their assigned partner, who listens while they respond to questions. After then, the couples trade places so that the second student can carry out the identical actions. After a while, the instructor only needs to remind the class to finish the turn-and-talk exercise on their own.

Prompts can have a variety of purposes, including the following:

• Practicing explaining text evidence to identify the problem (**pain**) answer questions

• Brainstorming to access background knowledge

• Answering a question related to key content

- Applying content to students' lives, creating meaningful connections

When you turn and talk to a partner, remember to...

- Tell your partner your answer in one to two sentences.
- Listen without interrupting while your partner tells you, their answer.
- Be kind and supportive so everyone feels comfortable sharing their answers.

The turn-and-talk routine consists of three basic steps.

Pair Students:

    1. Teacher provides a prompt. The teacher provides a brief written or spoken prompt.

    2. Partner 1 answers. Partner 1 responds to the prompt while Partner 2 listens.

    3. Partner 2 answers. Partner 2 responds to the prompt while Partner 1 listens.

The roles are reversed, and the second student answers the prompt while the first student listens.

The following are general guidelines for student pairing:

- Seat students who are respectful to each other side by side.
- Seat struggling learners next to students who are supportive.
- Seat less proficient English language learners next to more proficient English language learners

---

Challenges
One student talk too long and monopolizes the turn-and-talk sessions.
You notice a lot of off-task chatter.
A student with limited English proficiency struggles to participate in discussions.
You notice that some students are not paying attention to their partner.

Step 3. Classroom Collaboration/Shared Reading Review and Retell (Scheduled Time: 8 -10 minutes)

Framework for meaningful collaboration between students and students, between teachers and students.

Student instruction:

Share thinking come together to show information they learned from the poem. Students share their questions and answers. Students might concentrate on what they did not understand or did not know appropriately by talking about what they have already comprehended. These kinds of conversations can help students understand difficult text portions. Text analysis as the conversation in class moves from establishing facts to examining the text's more profound implications.

- **Shared Reading Review and Retell**

Use text to determine author's purpose

Prediction of what the poem is going to be about

Determine if the title appropriate for the poem

Identify and describe characters using key details

Determine if the poem is appropriate for classroom discussion

Encourage students to consider how they relate to the poem

Discuss student experiences around the topic

Discuss events directly related to the poem

• Essential Question - Sometimes you encounter difficult experiences in your life. What is an experience in your life that has been difficult?

- **Engage Thinking**

Ask students to read and talk about their ideas

Connect to knowledge

Use illustrations and text to determine the meaning of the poem

Create mental images

Describe how illustrations support a text

Summarize and synthesize

Improving Learning Abilities

• Discuss difficult emotions and identify them. Create a word bank of those emotions: anger, frustration, sadness, melancholy, heartache, loneliness, doubt, insecurity, etc.

- **Connect Illustration and Poem**

Examine illustrations

Interpret the illustrations

Describe how illustrations support poem

Discuss student opinion of the illustration

Discuss the details shown in the illustration

Connect illustration to personal experience

- **Social and Emotional Mindfulness**

Connect to experiences mine and others

Apply understanding or insight of student character

Apply understanding to build mindful knowledge

Put themselves in the shoes of the character and share a new point of view

Identify insight gained

Connection to experience

Comprehension – making connections

Building Positive Responses

How it may be useful in the school community

• Discuss with students how difficult experiences occur in our lives. Remind students that using grit and resilience can help overcome challenging obstacles. Have students brainstorm life experiences that connect to difficult emotions.

- **Connect Graph and Mindset Growth**

Examine graphs

Examine student response

Discuss comparisons and contrast

Discuss the details shown in the graph

Connect graphs to personal experience

Discuss insight gained from graph

Review the Mindset Building List on and Character Trait List

- **Promote a Positive Attitude:**

By developing mindful awareness and putting it into practice, students can cultivate a growth mindset, which will make them more capable of overcoming obstacles and realizing their full potential. Recall that developing a positive mindset is an ongoing process, and that maintaining these concepts over time is necessary to produce lasting effects.

- After each poetry lesson ask students which mindset vocabulary and character trait(s) it inspires them to use.

Poem: I Didn't Do Nothing

Author Goal: To make students aware of the importance of following school community rules despite if they perceive their actions as insignificant.

New Outlook: Encourage students to change students' perspective of rules, share and give reminders of how the rules are necessary for maintaining order and fairness in the classroom.

I Didn't Do Nothing

They said I did something
But I feel I did nothing
There are rules in school to keep order, peace, and protection
Now, I need to do a reflection
Let me see if I can make a connection

Do not speak without raising your hand
Do not get out of your seat without permission
Do not take anything without asking
Do not throw anything at or to someone
Do not hit anyone

I came to school.
First, I call out without raising my hand. Secondly, I get up out of my seat. Then, I took someone's pen and threw it at a student. Next, I hit the student sitting by me because he said something I didn't like. Lastly, I'm being sent to the principal's office and
I didn't do nothing
Why don't they stop this bluffing?

Insightful Questions

1) What is the main idea of the poem?

2) Can you relate to the student in the poem?

3) Do you like rules? Why or why not?

4) What are the benefits of this poem?

5) Fill in chart and discuss:

Rules	Actions

Conclusion

6) Do you think the students' actions should have changed? If so, when?

7) Did the poem cause you to change your thoughts about school rules? Explain

8) Reflect on the poem. How do you feel after reading it?

9) Did the student do anything wrong? Yes, or no? Describe the situation.

10) Does this poem change the way you feel about rules?

11) Is there a difference between breaking small rules and big rules?

12) How often should students review the rules?

13) Would it be a good idea for students to remind each other of the rules? Explain

14) Did the poem cause you to change your thoughts about school rules? Elaborate.

15) Describe your opinion of the last line of the poem?

Poem: First Day

Author objection: To illustrate what happens to some students on their first day of classes.

New Outlook: Encourage the student to adopt a more optimistic view and battled through their concerns by changing their perspective.

First Day

I got my hair done and it looks fine
And my clothes make me shine
To top it off I smell better than wine
I am ready to get on my grind
It is my first day of school and
<u>I feel like a fool</u>
<u>But I want to go and look cool</u>

<u>I am starting to feel sick</u>
The chair in front of me I want to kick
But everyone will know my name is Rick
<u>I feel like running off the bus,</u>
Surely, I cannot take all my stuff
I am not going to make a fuss
I will just sit here <u>feeling like I am in a rush</u>

<u>I am feeling more anxious</u>
I hope this is not contagious
I believe they may call it anxiety
<u>I cannot let this get the best of me entirely</u>
I will get myself together and
<u>Walk off this bus quietly with vitality</u>

Insightful Questions

1) Have you felt like this student on the first day of school?

2) What was the cause of the way the student was feeling?

3) What did you learn from this poem?

4) Fill in the chart. Compare and contrast.

You   Common   Student

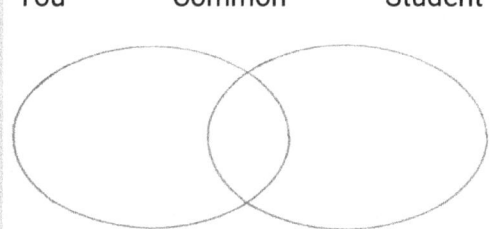

5) What emotions does the author cause you to feel?

6) Have you gained insight into the student's feelings? Describe.

7) After reading this poem could you reach out to a student who is sad or uncomfortable on the first day of school?

8) How does the shift at the end affect the overall message?

Poem: So Fast, So Fast

Goal of the author: To explain how some students are struggling readers, glide through tasks ignoring words they are unable to read.

New Outlook: Be supportive and encourage the student to take their time. Suggest they may need to pace themselves so they will have a better idea of how fast their reading. Remind students that asking for clarification from teachers or other students is acceptable if they don't understand something.

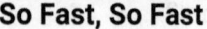

So Fast, So Fast

My mind and my heart smoothly move
So fast, so fast
<u>I wiz through my schoolwork</u>
So fast, so fast
I skip over words I cannot read
<u>I do not see details as I speed</u>
So, I can finish
So fast, so fast

<u>My teacher says review</u>
I do, and finish
So fast, so fast
<u>I ask, have I made many errors</u>.
She says yes, because
You wanted to get finished
So fast, so fast

It is time to fill out a job application
<u>I finished, so fast, so fast</u>
<u>I did not get an interview and wondered why?</u>
I was told, too many errors
Because you wanted to get finished
So fast, so fast…

Insightful Questions

1) What details in the poems help you identify the topic and the theme?

2) What's the author's intention?

3) Does this problem deserve attention? Explain.

4) What problem solving skills should the student have used?

5) Did the student see the effect of his behavior? Explain.

6) What happens because of the way the student responds to the problem?

7) In what stanza should the student have changed their mindset? Specify.

8) Should this poem help students gain a different point of view about rushing?

Poem: Discern

Author goal: To make clear how some students want to make wise decisions, but they lack the ability to recognize when they are making poor decisions.

New Outlook: Suggest the student consider reviewing the effects of past bad decisions and develop your problem-solving abilities.

Discern

I want to do what's right
So, I can seem so bright
But I can't see the light

I don't feel strong when everything comes out wrong
I have smarts and do my arts
When you ask me a question
I'll answer correctly without a suggestion

I can learn but I cannot discern
When I make a decision, it's not with precision
I turn down a hall only to run into a wall
I don't like trouble, but I always seem to fumble

I want to be straight but it's
Hard to concentrate
I don't want to be a problem child,
But it still takes me a while to learn

Considering it's hard for me to discern

Insightful Questions

1) What can happen because of the way the student responds?

2) Is this an informative poem?

3) How do you think the student should resolve their challenge?

4) Describe his feelings: sad, confused, or challenged.

5) Fill in the chart below and discuss:

6) Do you think this is a poem that should be discussed in class? Explain

7) What details in the poem do you identify with and why?

8) Would it be helpful for the student to review problem solving and solutions?

9) What does the student acknowledge at the end of the poem?

Poem: Hard

Author aims: To highlight students appear to be tough to protect themselves.

New Outlook: A hard disposition tone is characterized by a stern and unfriendly attitude. It can come across as harsh and unyielding, often lacking empathy or understanding. Remind the student that showing a friendly and approachable tone is not weakness. Everyone needs support sometimes.

Hard	Insightful Questions
<u>The hurt I feel</u> <u>Makes me not want to deal</u> <u>I will be wearing a shield</u> I know that I should kneel From the pain in my heart, I'll have to conceal <u>I have become cold,</u> So, I'm told Sadly, I feel like I'll fold <u>I must appear hard</u> <u>I am always on my guard</u> My mother always wants to act like she's my lifeguard Assuredly, she does not want me to end up in a graveyard <u>I go on with an empty hard heart</u> And dodge all those poisonous darts Hopefully, I will not depart Before I get a chance at a new start	1) What is the author's purpose? 2) How would you describe the student? 3) Could this be a real-life experience? Explain. 4) Can parents be important in a student's life? Describe. 6) Can you relate to the poem? Specify. 7) Do you think this is a significant poem? Explain. 8) Does the poem help you gain insight into the student's circumstances? 9) Do you think the student developed a different mindset? Describe.

Poem: Expression

Author purpose: To make students aware of how their unique style may define them.

New Outlook: Some may have a friendly and approachable tone, while others may come across as more serious and reserved. It is wise to let a student know if their style is interpreted negatively.

Expression

I like to do things my own way
This can be interpreted as a confession
<u>I have a hard time with my expressions</u>
Some of them make you want to question
If I am on a path of regression, profession or possession
<u>My speech, my behavior, my feelings, my reactions</u>
Are all styles of my expressions?
<u>However, they are displayed and determines my style</u>
And I say that with a smile
I apologize if they appear to be vile
You might want to take notes for my profile
Whatever you see please don't put it in my file
I hope that you stop building a case to put me on trial
I am always willing to reconcile
Sir, I don't want to add to the percentile
As you can see, I am only a juvenile

Insightful Questions

1) What is the significance of this poem? Describe.

2) Why do you think the author wrote this poem?

3) Describe the student.

4) Do the details help you understand the poem? Explain.

5) Do you identify with this student? Elaborate.

6) Can a student's expressions be misinterpreted?

7) Why does this poem provide a good learning experience?

8) What is the significance of the last line?

Poem: Twitch

Author's objective: To illustrate students twitch, or perhaps flitch and it can interfere with their ability to concentrate in class.

New Outlook: Avoid negative reactions to twitching students and allow extra time for their movements to settle before speaking, ensuring patience and allowing them to express themselves without feeling rushed.

Twitch

I twitch and twitch
And I flitch
You see me move

<u>Don't stop and stare</u>
I would love it if I could share
<u>It would help me eliminate my despair</u>
<u>You are probably unaware</u>
And you may say it's not fair,
I am not so rare

If I could stop
A twitch or flitch
I just might make a switch

Since moving is not always a choice
It's governed by an inside force
So, I hope you can be diverse

Insightful Questions

1) Does the student's experience happen in real life?

2) Is it a good idea to stop and stare at a student like the one in the poem?

3) What did the author want you to learn from the poem?

4) What could you do to help the student have high spirits in school?

5) If you could suggest to the student, what would it be and why?

6) Reflect on the poem. What have you learned?

7) Does this poem cause you to be mindful of students in your school community who are like the student? Explain

8) Does this poem change the way you view people who are not like you?

Poem: I Can't Help

Author's purpose: To give an example of how students might grow physically more quickly than peers their own age and may not be ready to learn what they are being taught.

New Outlook: Become a part of open and frequent communication between students. It is essential to be supportive in a consistent, supportive of an inclusive learning environment where it is crucial for students to feel comfortable working together.

I Can't Help

I got left back
I developed physically faster than students my age
Causing me to look larger for my age
Giving the notion I should know

I can't help
I am just not ready to learn what you are teaching me and
I can't remember what you just said
Or repeat it
I just don't understand

I can't help
I am not ready to learn what you are teaching
I maybe developmentally delayed
Causing me to be academically slower

I can't help
I am not ready to learn what you are teaching
I may graduate later than expected

I can't help I'm not ready to learn

I can't help
You, who have graduated on time
Have not learned how to understand and accept me...

Insightful Questions

1) What message does the author want you to know?

2) How do you think the student feels: anger, happiness, sadness, or depression? Explain.

3) Does the poem share informative information?

4) Fill each box and discuss:

1. Character	2. Setting
Theme	
Student Experiences	
Your Opinion	

5) Describe how you would feel if you were the student.

6) Reflect back on the poem. How do you feel after reading it?

7) Do you feel empathetic for the student? Why or why not?

Poem: My Child

<u>Author's concern</u>: To encourage students to be more conscious of their parents or care takers.

<u>New Outlook:</u> Share personal stories from your own life or from other students to help students understand and appreciate the different ways people can take care of them.

My Child

I love you
<u>My beautiful baby was born today</u>
How I can't wait to run and play
And to build figures out of clay.

Oh! No, they say it may be a delay
To my dismay
<u>In the hospital we may have to stay</u>

<u>Hooray! The doctors say everything is okay</u>
All I want to do is to hold it
Take care of it
I can't wait to teach it
Or babysit
<u>All I want to do is to love it</u>

My Child

Insightful Questions

1) What is the author's objective?

2) How does this parent feel about their baby?

3) What was the mother hoping to do with her baby?

4) Describe an important event from the poem and tell why it is important.

5) How does the title make you feel?

6) Does the mother in the poem remind you of someone you know?

7) Reflect back on the poem. How do you feel after reading it?

8) Do you think this poem can make readers feel happy, sad, or surprised

9) Why does this poem provide a good learning experience?

Poem: Get Him Back

Author goal: To make aware of the struggle of students who do not know how to handle when a student has hit them.

New Outlook: When a student is hit by another, it can be hard to accept. Encourage the student to seek help from a teacher or authority figure. Remind the student that violence is never the answer. Students can address the issue by working together towards building a more trusting and collaborative community within our school.

Get Him Back	Insightful Questions
When I go to school I wish that I were cool Students walk around me and say that I must think that I am a jewel <u>I must stand firm like a mule</u> They are trying to let me know that they will rule <u>Someone hits me and calls me out of my name</u> I ask myself is he or I insane They hate me because I am considered a brain How am I going to sustain? <u>All this misery and pain</u> <u>Every day it is making me feel drained</u> I don't want to be the blame <u>Feeling like getting him back</u> Nobody's listening that I was smacked <u>I am trying hard not to attack</u> What am I to do when all I think about is getting him back?	1) Is it acceptable to hit a student in your school community? Explain. 2) Describe the student's reaction? 3) Why do you think the author created this poem? 4) How would you feel if you were the student? 5) Should the student talk to adults before things escalate? 6) Does it remind you of something you have experienced in real life? 7) Was the student considered strong or weak for not retaliating? Elaborate. 8) What could you say to the student to show you understand what they're experiencing?

Poem: The Way, I See It

Author's purpose: To give an account on how common it is for students to see, interpret and write letters and numbers backwards.

New Outlook: It is important to be supportive and encourage the student to understand their strengths and weaknesses, encouraging them to reach their full potential.

The Way, I See It

When you ask me to read?
I cannot see the "b"
<u>The way you see it</u>
It looks like a "d"

I cannot see a "n"
The way you see it
It looks like a "u"

I cannot see a "q"
The way you see it
It looks like a "p"

I cannot see a "3"
The way you see it
It looks like an "8"

I cannot see a "6"
The way you do It
It looks like a "9"

Who knew what I see is not the way I should see it?
What I see is the way I see it

<u>The Reverse</u>
This can make it hard to converse
Sorrowfully,
I plead do not let this be a curse!
Since there are many like me on this universe

Insightful Questions

1) Do you know anyone who sees things like the student in the poem?

2) What is the author's objective?

3) Does this poem change the way you view students who see letters differently?

4) Complete the chart. Compare and discuss:

What do you know?	What have you learned?	How can you help
_____	_____	_____
_____	_____	_____

5) Can this poem prompt you to assist students who are like the student in the poem?

6) Can the way the student sees affect his reading or math? Explain.

7) What emotions does the author cause you to feel?

8) At the end, does the student create their own positive mindset?

Uplifting The Pain...Growth Mindset

Poem: I scream, I fight, I'm mad

Author's purpose: To make aware how students sometimes feel the need to express themselves by screaming, crying and fighting.

New Outlook: Encourage the student to find positive outlets and coping mechanisms, like journaling, art, sports, or talking to trusted friends.

I scream, I fight, I'm mad

Unfortunately,
<u>I need to let off some steam</u>
This is not a dream
I'm not on your team
I am feeling so mean
<u>All I want to do is scream</u>

<u>I'll fight with all my might</u>
Things are getting so uptight
You'd better get out of my sight
Before I put you in twilight
I need the light

Regrettably,
<u>I'm so mad</u>
Constantly, I feel so sad
People tell me I won't be a grad
Evidently, this is not a fad
All because I want my dad
I hope one day to be glad
For its truly miserable to act bad

Insightful Questions

1) Have you experienced strong emotions you could not control?

2) What does the author want you to think about?

3) How could you personally help the student to feel better?

4) Is the reason for the student's behavior valid? Explain.

5) How can a student's behavior get re-directed in class? Describe.

6) How does the student feel at the end of the poem?

7) Does the last line reveal that the student is trying to excuse their behavior?

Poem: My Father Figure

Goal of the author: To convey how students want a positive father figure.

New Outlook: Point out there may be other positive male role models that they can look up to. This could be an uncle, grandfather, family friend, or even a male teacher or coach. Remember to be patient and understanding.

My Father Figure

Father figure
Provides paternal functions
Authoritative while exhibiting strength
Powerful and protective
Extends energy when I need to get checked
Especially, if I appear like a suspect

A positive father figure whom I can look up to
Making me feel brand new
Stays around to deliver
A father figure who
Treats me like I'm their child
And not just for awhile

Someone who I can become attached
And be well matched
Sensitive to my emotional and physical needs
Especially if I feel anxiety or grief
Providing comforting relief

Shape my thinking as I find myself
Explain how I'm feeling
While correcting my dealings
Sharing my concealing

Gives directions and helps me find my path
Looks out on my behalf
Adds happiness and makes me laugh
Just Loves me
A substitute for a biological father
For example, a loving adoptive father,
stepfather, grandparent, older
brother, or teacher

Insightful Questions

1) What is the author's objective?

2) Identify the problem and solution of the poem?

3) What emotions is the student feeling? Elaborate.

4) How do you feel after reading the poem? Describe.

5) Can you identify with the student? Specify.

6) Why does this poem provide a good learning experience?

7) What parts of the poem are more important to you?

Poem: Clean

Author's purpose: To share that there are students who constantly seek to ensure that their surroundings are clean and organized.

New Outlook: As a trusted classmate, suggest different topics that make the student happy to distract them from thinking about whether things are clean and organized.

Clean!

Most things make me feel mean
Because they seem to be unclean

Is it clean?
I want to sit in a chair,
But I won't dare

I want to lie down
But I'll just make a frown

Do you have a new or clean dish?
How I wish

Turn off the water knobs
Please don't think I'm a snob

Hold my hand
No, I'd rather make fans

I want things in order
And I wish that had a recorder

The house is in a dismay
Maybe someone needs to spray

Where did you get this from?
Don't look so dumb

Did my coat touch the floor?
Then I don't want it anymore

Is that a black spot?
Then I must not
Is it clean?

What do you mean?

Is it clean?
I hate to be this extreme

Insightful Questions

1) Did personal experiences come to mind as you read the poem? Describe

2) What does the author want you to think about?

3) Can you relate to the student? Specify.

4) Explain the significance of the poem.

5) What does the author want you to think about?

6) Is it important to learn about students in your school community? Elaborate.

Poem: Focus

Author's purpose: To describe how students get ready for listening and taking in the material, but it is challenging to pay attention.

New Outlook: With time and effort, you can be instrumental in supporting an inclusive classroom that develops better focus and concentration skills. It is essential for students to be patient and understanding while trying different strategies to help students focus.

Focus

I sit down to listen and learn
But my mind is moving so fast
I twist and turn
I am trying to pay attention
As I try to group the information
What is she saying?
I ask myself to
Focus, focus

I am thinking about this
And I am thinking about that
I try to pay attention and focus
You call on me and I am off focus
What am I thinking?
Focus, focus

There are ways and remedies
Out there which can slow my
Mind down, so I can
Focus, focus

Frantically, I ask "what do I do?"
"How am I to learn?"
When I cannot
Focus, focus

My friends have reached out
Discouraging my self-doubt
Now, I won't have to pout

Take notice
That one day I will
Focus, focus

Insightful Questions

1) What does the author want you to learn from this poem?

2) Can you identify with this poem? How?

3) Can the student solve their problem? Explain.

4) Is this an insightful poem which deserves attention? Describe.

5) Is the message in this poem important? Specify.

6) What would you suggest to this student?

7) Do you know students who have the same complaint?

Poem: Hunger

Author's objective: To make aware there are students in need of food and their hunger drove them to act in an unexpected way.

New Outlook: Speak consolably to the student privately to see if you can suggest the student speaks to their teacher or counselor.

Hunger

I remember when I was younger
I experience such great hunger
I often stopped to wonder
Because I felt like a stranger
We had to lookout for danger

Not having made me so mad
I quickly became so sad
My youth didn't last
All things considered, I had to grow up so fast

Where I lived was in the hood
Patiently in my doorway I stood
I had to go out to get some food

Am I a thief?
There is so much disbelief
I used to be silent
I never became violent
Still life's needs put me in crime
That's not fine

All I want to do is strive
While I try to survive

Insightful Questions

1) Did the author create a significant poem that should be discussed?

2) Are all opportunities good ones?

3) Explain how the student could be helped?

4) Is it important to think before you act? Explain.

5) Does the student exhibit a learned behavior? Describe.

6) Who was responsible for the student's actions?

7) Does survival dictate the course of actions you choose? Explain.

8) Describe your opinion of the last line of the poem?

Poem: Sway

Author's purpose: To highlight there are students who will go through great lengths to have to create division.

New Outlook: Encourage open communication, talk. Make the student feel comfortable expressing their thoughts and feelings. This will help them feel heard and understood and may reduce their need to manipulate situations.

Sway

<u>She likes to get her way</u>
<u>She tells things to make them sway</u>
She may take a day
<u>She acts like she's in a play</u>
She'll get upset and cry

She'll say things that will make them want to fly
<u>The people believe her and follow her sigh</u>
They don't verify to see if it's a lie
Discouraging words, she uses will fortify
A method you cannot deny

Consequently, they get very uptight
<u>Until they want to fight</u>
<u>And no one wants to reunite</u>
As she pretends to be so upright even polite
And that's just not right

Insightful Questions

1) What line supports the title of the poem?

2) Does the student's behavior happen in real life?

3) Why did the author create this poem?

4) Is this student concerned about the results of her actions?

5) Why does this poem provide a good learning experience?

6) Describe the behavior progression: Review student behavior chart and discuss: (line 2, 7, and 12)

Beginning   Middle   End

7) Can the student cause others to follow her, creating division? Specify.

8) Should you avoid circumstances that do not cause a peaceful outcome for students? Explain.

9) After reading this poem, do you appreciate the value of sharing student unity in our schools and communities? Describe.

10) What would you suggest to this student?

Poem: I Don't Trust

Author's purpose: To share there are students who lack interpersonal trust. They are uncomfortable with what someone you say to them.

New Outlook: Participate in promoting honesty, empathy, understanding school community

I Don't Trust

<u>I don't trust</u>
The way you <u>look at me</u>
The things you <u>say to me</u>
The things you <u>do to me</u>

I don't trust
Why are you going to the store?
Why didn't you shut the door?
Were you going to push me to the floor?

I don't trust
<u>Were you talking about me</u>?
This just doesn't feel right you see
Seriously, don't try to pour me some tea

I don't trust don't you agree?

Insightful Questions

1) What does the author want students to learn from this poem?

2) What do you know about the topic of this poem?

3) Why is the title appropriate for this poem?

4) Does this poem affect you personally when you read it? Describe.

5) Has your viewpoint changed toward students who express themselves like the student? Explain.

6) Do you feel like the student in this poem? Specify.

7) How can you get along with a student like the one in the poem?

8) After reading the poem, what can you conclude about the student?

9) If you were the student, would you want someone to reach out to you? Explain.

Poem: Stutter

Author's objective: To emphasize sometimes students have a difficult time pronouncing words smoothly.

New Outlook: It's important to avoid negative reactions such as laughing or making fun of a student who stutters. Allow extra time to verbally express themselves. Be patient and give them the time they need to communicate without feeling rushed.

Stutter

I stutter
<u>When I'm about to speak, it makes me shutter</u>
I want to melt like butter
I can speak but it comes out like an utter
I talk about it constantly with my mother
She says some encouraging words to help me recover
<u>When I must speak, I want to become a runner</u>
Or maybe a drummer

Since I stutter
<u>I feel like butterflies are in my stomach want to flutter</u>
I just look off in a wonder
Every time I try it seems rougher
I don't want to try to talk again just to blunder
It's important I become tougher
Surely, I won't continue to suffer just
Because I stutter

Insightful Questions

1) If a student had difficulties speaking fluently, how would you react?

2) How would you feel if you were like the student in the poem?

3) Does the topic poem relate to you?

4) What is the author's purpose?

5) What have you learned? Specify.

6) How could you assist a student who has difficulty explaining themselves in school?

7) When you read this poem, what pictures did you see in your head?

8) Did the poem help you gain a better insight into the student's problem? How?

9) At the end of the poem, what do you notice about the student?

Poem: Here, There and Everywhere

Author's purpose: To emphasize that there are students who are energetic and incredibly fidgety. It is possible to mix things up or forget things.

New Outlook: It's critical to interact with the student and understand their viewpoint. Continue extending understanding and empathy among the inclusive school community.

Here, There and Everywhere

Some don't know what to think
As a child it causes you <u>to have plenty</u> of energy
You feel so fidgety

You may <u>answer out of turn</u>
Then you just want to squirm
You may <u>get matters mixed up</u>
And you'll have to get them fixed up

<u>You may forget things</u>
While you wish that you had wings
<u>You try to focus on a topic</u>
You tell yourself stop it

<u>As you're talking your mind may switch</u>
And you're unhitched or
You'll be looking all around
But you won't make a sound

<u>It may cause you to lose things</u>
Too bad they don't have any strings

You may put <u>something down</u>
<u>Forget</u> and just make a frown
You may be eating at the table
Suddenly, <u>you'll get up</u> and end up in the stable

<u>Forgetting your thoughts during a conversation</u>
Can make you feel some aggravation

Insightful Questions

1) What do you already know about the topic?

2) What does the author want students to learn from this poem?

3) Does the poem provide insight into the student's uniqueness? Explain.

4) Fill in the chart. Compare and discuss:

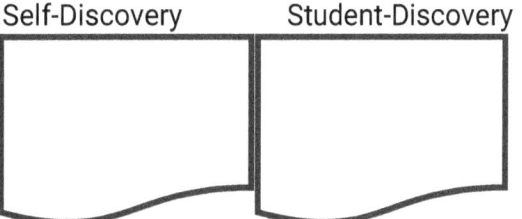

Self-Discovery   Student-Discovery

5) Can you relate to the student? Specify.

6) Describe what personal experiences come to mind as you read the poem?

7) Explain how the students' action has on their attitude at the end?

8) After reading the poem, have you gained insight? Elaborate

9) Why is it important to learn about students in your school community?

Poem: Explode

<u>Author's purpose</u>: To shed light on students' perspective can shift because of the extreme pressure and fruitless attempts.

<u>New Outlook</u>: Share with the students that deep breathing may help. Offer support in letting them know that they are not alone in your struggles, and there are people in the school community who are concerned about their welfare.

Explode

What should I do?
<u>When there is so much pressure</u>
I don't want to become an aggressor

<u>With all my failing endeavors</u>
My head is feeling like it is in a compressor
<u>I have changed my thoughts because</u>
I don't want to become a depressor
I'm starting to feel like I'm lessor
I might need to seek a confessor

<u>To talk about positive thoughts</u>
I'd like to <u>become a progressor</u> or
Perhaps I'll go to school to see a professor
So, one day I'll be a successor

Insightful Questions

1) Why do you think the author chose the title?

2) Describe the student's feelings.

3) How does the poem make you feel? Describe.

4) Do you think the student could have avoided their reaction?

5) What inference solutions should the student try? Specify.

6) Do you think there are students who feel like the student? Explain.

7) What would you suggest to a student who faces challenges like the student?

8) Can sharing calming strategies with the class be helpful?

9) Would discussing the student's triggers be helpful? Specify.

10) What steps would you take to gain control if you felt like the student?

Uplifting The Pain...Growth Mindset

Poem: Expectation

Author's purpose: To reveal some students are viewed with suspicion. As such, they anticipate that they will be impolite.

New Outlook: We must not judge people by their appearance. Students can elevate their behavior levels and maintain a positive and respectful learning environment.

Expectation

When you see me

You never know what to expect

At first people see me as a suspect

Consequently, they expect me to disrespect

I won't do anything I will regret

Sometimes I don't give a heck

Absolutely, I will not accept

I will just have to reflect

On the good and the bad deflect

Taking in account my expectation

I promise I will not neglect

To give you

Respect in every aspect

Insightful Questions

1) Does this student have a positive attitude?

2) Do you judge someone who speaks differently than you?

3) How do you think a student acts if they are perceived as trouble? Describe.

4) Should a student be respected if they avoid getting into trouble? Explain.

5) Fill in the chart. Compare and discuss:

   Self-Perception   Student-Perception

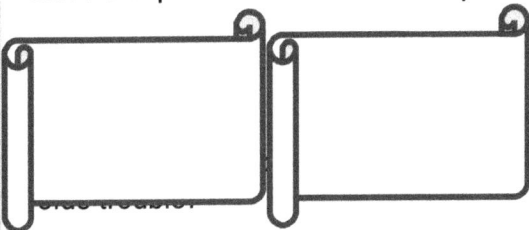

7) How does the student perceive oneself?

8) Does this poem cause you to have a positive mindset towards students and teachers in your school community? Explain.

9) Should the message in this poem be shared with others?

10) Why is the last line commendable?

Poem: Don't Touch

Author's purpose: To highlight there are students who need help with wanting things that do not belong to them.

New Outlook: You can share with the student that although you might occasionally feel inclined to borrow what you need, taking something without permission is never appropriate.

Don't Touch

I see his toy
I see her pencil
I see mom's quarter
I see some candy

It doesn't belong to me
Don't take, don't take
I want that cell phone
I want those shoes
I want some money
I want a car

It doesn't belong to me
Don't take, don't take
I took her money
I took his cell phone
I took a car

I jacked or stole from them all
And now I must take the fall
Because

I should have listened to myself
"It doesn't belong to me"
"Don't take, don't take things that don't belong to me"

Insightful Questions

1) What does the author want students to learn from this poem?

2) Can you relate to this poem? Specify.

3) Describe how your personal knowledge affects you when you read the poem?

4) Is it okay for a student to take something that does not belong to them?

5) Does the poem give you a different insight on the student's behavior? Explain.

6) Why does this poem provide a good learning experience?

7) At any time did the student's perspective change? Describe.

8) Could positive student interaction discourage students from taking from other students?

Uplifting The Pain...Growth Mindset

Poem: You Yell

Aim of the author: To share that some students receive redirection before coming to school.

New Outlook: Greeting students with a smile and a kind word, setting the tone for a great day ahead.

You Yell

If I ask you a question
If I touch something
If I don't move as fast as you like
When you tell me to sit down
When you tell me to shut up

Before I go to school
You yelled at me making me feel like a fool
All I hear is constant ridicule
Making me feel like a minuscule
Emotionally, it feels cruel

Bringing me down is feeling uncool
and sad all day long
Hoping that it does not become my theme song

During class I asked a student for a pencil
I said please
But he didn't respond
As a result, I
Got into trouble for yelling at him
Deep down I want to cry

I hate that I must suppress
Being in suspense
Feeling vexed
Or wishing that I were somewhere else

All I have for you is gratitude
And love in a multitude

Insightful Questions

1) What is the author's objective?

2) What are reasons why this poem provides a good learning experience?

3) Can you make a connection with the student? Explain.

4) How was the student affected by his experience? Describe.

5) Does this poem cause you to understand the state of mind of students in your school community? Elaborate.

6) Do you think the student refocuses their spirit?

Poem: Never Wrong

Author's purpose: To show how students are exclusively focused on being correct and having correct answers.

New Outlook: Remember, being wrong is not a sign of weakness, but rather an opportunity to learn and grow. Enlighten the student instead of constantly striving to be right, focus on being open to new ideas and learning from your mistakes.

Never Wrong

During school, if I got something wrong
It made me feel like I did not belong
If an incorrect answer is marked in red or with an X
That would make me get so vexed

Therefore, the only ones that I got right were marked with a check
Allowing If an incorrect answer is marked in red or with an X
That would make me get so vexed

Causing me to feel great and smart

No criticisms, positive suggestions or corrections are accepted
They are all interpreted in a negative direction
Making me feel rejection

If I don't agree
I distort my perception
Then it doesn't seem like deception
It is more like a diversion

Pushing blame from me
If I'm asked, "Did you do well?"
I answer "Yes" to circumvent any contrary reactions

If I go to the store and
I bring back the wrong thing

Of course, I must have been given the incorrect name

Never admitting an error

Insightful Questions

1) What is the main message in this poem?

2) Is it possible to never be wrong? Clarify.

3) Does this poem provide good reasons to do periodic self-reflection?

4) Should students say things to make them appear better than others? Explain.

5) When wrong, is it wise to deflect the blame from you onto someone else?

6) Is this a poem that should be discussed with your classmates? Elaborate.

7) Can encouraging positive student interaction help student outlook? How?

Because it is like an act of terror
So do not ask me any questions
Because it is hard to give a clear confession

Poem: Slow

Author's purpose: To reveal how students struggle to keep up with the pace of things.

New Outlook: Presenting a positive and welcoming understanding tone can cause students to feel more confident. Your continued student support is crucial for students to feel comfortable and motivated to continue learning at their own pace.

Slow

I am slow
I just can't keep up with the flow
You talk to me but
I just don't know

Don't call me slow

When I don't understand
It feels like a blow
One day, I just want to show
I'm not slow

I would like to keep up
As I grow
And become a Pro

Now in training to learn a new skill
To increase my cash flow
To avoid a fur low
I am still learning slowly
Unfortunately, everyone knows
But once I got it
I got it...
A new job

Now, I don't feel slow no Mo
And I can smile with a glow!

Insightful Questions

1) What is the author's purpose?

2) What do you think the poem reveals?

3) Does the student's experience happen in real life?

4) Does the poem give your insight on this topic?

5) Do you know anyone who feels like the student in the poem?

6) How could you help a student who feels like the student?

7) At the end, does the student create a new self-concept? Describe.

Poem: My Hair

Author's purpose: The student's hair causes her discomfort. Her hair wasn't combed, and she feels such despair.

New Outlook: Encourage her to speak to her parents about how she feels about her hair. Let the student know that you are aware of how important it is to feel confident and comfortable in your appearance in school. Perhaps working together to find a solution that makes her feel more comfortable about her hair style.

My Hair

My hair wasn't combed today
Desperately, I want to go out and stay!

My Hair
This isn't going to fly
It has not been styled for a while
Unfortunately, it seems like it's my lifestyle

My Hair
These words I share
Because I feel such despair
It is so unfair
My hair I don't want to wear

Long and stringy or
Short and Dry
Making me not care!

My hair
Don't you dare!
Stop and look at me in a glare
I want to get out of this square
Sometimes all I can say is beware

When I get grown
I will fix my hair
Then they will stop and stare
Because my hair will a stylish flair
Making me feel like a millionaire

Insightful Questions

1) What does the author want you to know?

2) As you are reading this poem, what does it cause you think of?

3) Why is this poem important?

4) Do you know a student whose behavior was misunderstood because of their hair consciousness?

5) Fill in the chart. Compare and discuss:

What you know   What you have Learned

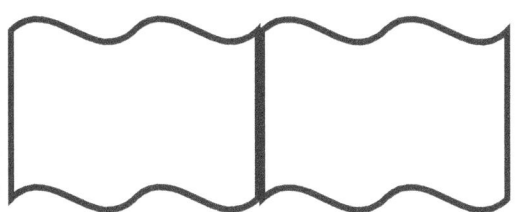

6) How would you have felt if you were the student?

7) What do you say to a student who wears a head cover because of their hair concerns?

8) Has the poem helped you to understand the students' anxieties?

Poem: Sound

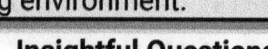

Author's goal: To illustrate how some students express themselves solely through sounds and possibly words. They may struggle with social relationships, communication, and sensory processing.

New Outlook: It is important to approach autistic students with tolerance, compassion, and understanding. Be patient with their communication skills. For them to flourish, participate in creating a calm safe and encouraging environment.

Sound

When I speak
Sometimes, all I can do is make a shriek
Some think I'm a freak
The future can look so bleak

may seem mystique
But
Profoundly, I am unique
At time I feel like taking a leap
But I can be as mild as a sheep

I want to confess
I can read, add and write
But I can't express myself, verbally
How I wish I could

Then I would speak what's on my mind
So please be kind
I can be defined
As a part of mankind

All I can do is make a sound
Since a cure they have not found
And's profound

Insightful Questions

1) What did the author want you to learn from the poem?

2) If a student does not smile, laugh, or show emotions, how should you communicate with them?

3) Do you make fun of someone's behavior if you do not understand it? Explain.

4) If you are trying to be friends with a student and they do not respond, what should you do?

5) How can you make a student feel welcome if they do not communicate with you verbally? Describe.

6) Which stanza is most impacting to you?

Poem: Size Me

Author's purpose: To give an account of how students are unhappy with their appearance.

New Outlook: Avoid making comments about appearance and instead focus on praising students for their efforts and achievements. Encourage the student to have positive self-talk and focus on their strengths and unique qualities. Promote the importance of self-acceptance and self-care rather than focusing on weight or appearance.

Size Me

Why are you looking at me?
Just hear my plea
Don't make me want to flee
Hope you will agree

My appearance I cannot help
I just want you to know
How I felt
Since you haven't dealt
Sometimes it makes me want to melt

My size
Makes me want to put on a disguise
Since no one sees my outcries

I like to eat
Because it soothes my butterflies
Or uneasy quizzes feeling

So, stop your scrutinize
Instead, you should apologize

I'm a fill-size
I want you to recognize
I don't have to slenderize
Or exercise
To legitimize...me

Insightful Questions

1) What is your opinion of this poem?

2) Do you know someone like the student in this poem? Describe.

3) If you were in the poem, what would your relation be to the student?

4) Do you think there are students who feel like this student?

5) How did the student feel because of the circumstances?

6) Have you come to school feeling like the student in the poem? Specify.

7) Can you understand the student?

8) Does the student's perspective change for the best?

Poem: Just Read

Author's purpose: To reveal the feelings of students struggling with reading, comprehending, and interpreting material.

New Outlook: Empathetically and supportively approach students struggling with reading, encouraging them to seek help when needed and to seek clarification from teachers or classmates.

Just Read

How dare you tell me to
Just Read

<u>Painfully I plead,
I CAN'T READ!</u>

I look at what I see
But I still don't have the key

I Can't Read

All the answers are supposed to come from what I read
So, one day I can supersede

<u>I cannot read</u>
Many want to disagree
Making me feel like a lessee

Where can this lead?
I do not want to continue to feel like this is a misdeed
I do not want to sow this seed

<u>All I want to be is freed
From this disappointing deed</u>

Daily I plead to be determined to just read,
And eagerly anticipating indeed

I WILL LEARN TO READ AT MY OWN SPEED
And SUCCEED!

Insightful Questions

1) What does the author want you to learn from this poem?

2) How do you think the student feels: angry, happy, sad, or depressed?

3) Should the student ask for help?

4) Do you know any students who feel like the student in the poem?

5) Does the poem cause you to feel empathy for the student? Describe.

6) How do you think the student feels in the beginning and the ending? Explain.

Poem: She Thinks She's Cute

Author's purpose: According to a student's assessment, another student presents herself as superior.

New Outlook: Focus on building genuine connections and relationships with others and letting your personality shine. Do not jump to conclusions without knowing the facts.

She Thinks She's Cute

She thinks she is cute
Comparing her to the forbidden fruit
I don't give a hoot.
They say she has a lot of loot
Who cares when her face looks like a boot
She acts like she's better
Like she's a trendsetter
She does her work with such vigor
I begin to feel very bitter
Making me want to hit her
Or trip her
So, I wrote her a personal letter
My bad to my surprise, she's just a confident go getter.

Making me reconsider
Since the problem was my lack of control lever
Because I should know better
I made a gross error

Insightful Questions

1) Is this a poem that should be discussed in class? Specify.

2) What happened because the student's style is misinterpreted?

3) Is it important to recognize if one's thinking is creating a problem, and then reevaluate them in reality? Elaborate.

4) What steps should the student have taken to stop negative thoughts?
Fill in the chart. Compare and discuss: Use inferences.

5) What does the student acknowledge at the end of the poem?

6) What have you learned to help you evaluate your thoughts and not to jump to conclusions?

Poem: My Mom

Aim of the author: To discuss how students believe their mom is special and that no one else like her.

New Outlook: If you have a good relationship with your mom, you can share your own experiences with other students. This can help other students see that they are not alone in feeling grateful for their mom, and it can also give them a different perspective on mother-child relationships.

My Mom

Mothers, mommas, aunties, big mommas, sisters, step mommas
<u>Thank you for being here</u>
<u>Even though it seems like I keep you in the rear</u>
But my feelings are sheer
The thought of you not being here
Brings me great fear
Although I'm a teen I will shed a tear
<u>Remembering the late nights, you persevere</u>
I am sincere

I thank you for
Times you stayed up with me at night
Times that you had to come up to my school
Times that you went to work to make sure that we had food and clothing
Times that <u>you made sure that we went to school</u>
Times that you tried to help me

I can't say enough
Because I know that it's tough
I know there are times that you wanted to huff and puff
Especially when things looked rough

I thank you for being adaptable
There's no one comparable
You're valuable

Insightful Questions

1) How does the student feel?

2) Does the student's experience happen in real life?

3) Reflect on the title. Do you think it is appropriate?

4) How do you feel after reading the poem? Describe.

5) What emotions is the student feeling? Explain.

6) Why does this poem provide a good learning experience?

7) How does the poem help you gain insight into the student's circumstances?

8) Does this poem relate to you or your family? How?

Poem: Down Hearted

Author's purpose: To explain why It appears when students are not moving forward, they may be weary of feeling oppressed, lacking both strength and interest.

New Outlook: Remember to be patient and understanding with the student. Let them know that you are there for them and that they are not alone. With your support and encouragement, they may be able to overcome their feelings of sadness and feel better.

Down Hearted

I look a mess
I feel less
I have not had any rest
It is hard to be at my best
My problems I want them addressed
It seems like I am not making any progress

I don't even want to get dressed
I have no strength or interest I confess
My heart is racing in my chest
My brain feels obsessed

I am glad that you have given me this opportunity to distress
Preventing my feelings from becoming compressed
I am tired of feeling oppressed
It is undesirable to become stressed
Instead, I prefer to detest it
Understandingly, there are so many of us who are depressed
I thank you for listening, now I can avoid becoming hard-pressed

Insightful Questions

1) Does this poem change the way you view people?

2) Is the repetitious word "I" significant in how the student is feeling? Specify.

3) If a student is not available, is it advisable to seek an adult? Explain.

4) What is your opinion of the way the students managed the problem? Describe.

5) What is the main conflict that the student in the poem faces?

6) Reflect back on the poem, what have you learned?

7) Why does this poem provide a good learning experience?

8) Do you think that it is important for students to listen to each other in school in their school community? Explain.

Poem: Out My Name

<u>Author's purpose:</u> To give an account of what happens when a student is called a name.

<u>New Outlook:</u> Encourage students to lift each other up and celebrate their differences. This can help create a more inclusive and supportive environment for all students.

Out My Name

<u>You called me out my name</u>
This is no game
I can't stand that because
<u>It drives me insane</u>
If necessary, I will have you tamed
Or I'll take you out of your frame

Outside it appears
I have a hard cover
<u>I don't want you to discover</u>
Deep down inside
<u>I feel soft or awkward</u>
So, I don't want it to be revealed or
<u>Make me feel shame</u>

Don't get it twisted
Because I don't care if you
Tell the teacher
She's just acts like a preacher

However, you'd better watch your mouth
I don't know who you think
you are
Since you are always acting bizarre

I'm not with that dissing stuff
I can tell that you are not that tough
It's just a part of your fluff

Insightful Questions

1) What is the main conflict the student faces?

2) As you are reading the poem, what does it make you think of?

3) Why is this poem important to discuss in class?

4) Can you relate to the student? Describe.

5) How would you have felt if you were the student?

6) What is the lesson learned in the poem?

7) Is this poem based on misunderstanding among classmates? Explain.

8) How does the student's disposition change at the end?

Poem: Clumsy

Author's goal: To share that students can be clumsy

New Outlook: Remind them to slow down and be more mindful of their movements and pay attention to their surroundings. Encourage them to keep a positive attitude and to not let their circumstances define them.

Clumsy

I broke my toe
Fell and hit the flo

Then, I went walking and slipped
Turned around and then I flipped
Now, I feel so whipped

It got late so I dipped
Now, I feel like I've been whipped
I tried to run fast, and my pants ripped

Only to be tripped
Thus, chipped my tooth,
Slit my lip and fell on my hip

Boy, I've got to get a grip
Next time, I'll try to be equipped

Insightful Questions

1) Reflect on the title. Do you think it was appropriate?

2) Highlight what you notice about the student?

3) Have you experienced a clumsy moment? Describe.

4) How would you have reacted if you were the student?

5) Describe what you were imagining as you read the poem?

6) What does the author want you to know?

7) If you could make a suggestion to the student, what would it be?

8) Can you connect with the student? Specify.

Poem: Bully

<u>Author's purpose</u>: To illustrate how bullies act discreetly because they don't want other people to realize that they are bullies.

<u>New Outlook</u>: Make it clear to students that bullying behavior is not allowed on any level. Offer the students being bullied need positive encouragement. Be supportive of non-judgmental and inclusive school communities that are understanding.

Bully

You scream and holler
You use profanity
You are puffed up
You talk down to others

You make threats
Trying to make people sweat
Walking around trying to make everyone upset

You whisper
Don't make a sound
You want to make sure no one's around
You are scared to be found

It is terrible
You want to make me frown
Then you want me to look down
To make me feel like a clown

Now
You don't want me to tell
I can't let you put me in a shell
Truthfully, if you don't stop

I'LL TELL
YOU BULLY!

Insightful Questions

1) After reading this poem, how do you feel about bullies?

2) Does the bully make the student feel sad or happy, and explain?

3) What would you do if you met a student like the bully? Describe.

4) Fill in the chart. Describe the Bully's characteristics in each stanza in the boxes 1-4 and discuss:

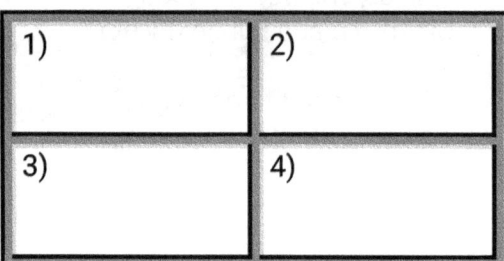

5) What are two things you learned?

6) Was the problem resolved? Describe.

7) How can you help a student who is getting bullied?

8) Has this poem changed your opinion of a bully?

9) What is your opinion of the last 2 lines?

10) If you are being bullied, should you suffer in silence? Elaborate.

Poem: Math

Author's aims: To give information about students finding it difficult to work with numerical expressions, patterns and would much rather do other things.

New Outlook: Remind students that it's okay to ask for help when they don't understand something. Encourage them to reach out to their teachers or classmates for clarification.

Math

I can't do math
Don't you laugh

I'd rather go out and dance
I'd just like a chance

To do math
I have trouble with numbers
I can't get the patterns
It might not matter

More and less, and larger and smaller
How should I comprehend?
Since this way I can't win

I have trouble with number patterns
Add, subtract, multiply or division
All look like a collision

How to learn the relationships between single items and groups
This is going to make me jump through hoops

How do I remember symbols?
Or the quantity they represent

All of it doesn't make any cents...
I do not want to become content
Because one day I want to be able to count dividends

Insightful Questions

1) What are the benefits of this poem?

2) What is the author's goal?

3) How does the student respond to their problem?

4) How do you think the student feels: anger, excitement, happiness, sadness, or disappointment?

5) Should the student ask for help?

6) What happens because of the student's actions?

7) Does this poem enhance awareness of this student's dilemma?

8) How can you be encouraging to the student?

Poem: Answers Right

Author's purpose: To reveal there are times when a teacher calls on the student who is talking, getting up from their seat, or wandering around, the student responds correctly.

New Outlook: Try to catch students when they are paying attention and following directions. Offer praise and acknowledge their efforts to encourage them to continue that behavior

Answers Right

<u>Whether I'm out of my seat, walking, talking,</u>
or playing around in class without permission
The teacher will call on me for an answer and
I get it right

<u>They say it's because I'm smart</u>
But I never feel apart
The teacher automatically
Prepares others for me to bogart

Or say something wrong from my mouth part
It makes me feel like I should opt out
What I need is a fresh start
<u>Or a jumpstart</u>

No one would believe
Underneath I have bleeding heart
I wish I could have a heart to heart
To release the cause of this black heart

Where should I start
Since deep down I know I am smart
I can take advantage of head start
While I ignore anyone who wants to distort
Because I don't want to fall apart

Now, I've made my decision to restart
<u>I'll follow my own flow chart</u>
Everyone is going to be surprised I've stopped
And won't revert
But
<u>Making an A in academics and behavior</u>

Insightful Questions

1) What is the author's purpose?

2) Describe the stages of the student's self-discovery.

3) Describe the behavior progression:
Review student behavior chart and discuss: (line 1, 11, 22 and 26)

Beginning   Middle   End

4) Is this an inspiring poem? Specify.

5) How does the student feel at the end of the poem?

6) Can you identify with the student?

7) How does the student's mindset growth affect you?

Poem: Why I Don't Try

Author's attention: To share student differences but are not necessarily limitations.

New Outlook: Be active in creating a supportive in an inclusive learning environment. Help student to recognize their strengths, encouraging them to strive to reach their full potential. Be patient and urge them to study their classwork carefully and take their time.

Why I Don't Try	Insightful Questions
I speak differently I hear differently I think differently I write differently I see differently I behave differently <u>So, I don't try</u> As I speak, I stutter As I listen, I don't hear sounds As I think, I can't think clearly As I write, I write upside down As I see, I see things backwards As I sit, I can't sit still <u>So, I don't try</u> I don't try Because I am afraid of myself The pain I may feel I don't try because I'm scared Scared of what you may do, say or think of my differences as Limitations Tearfully, I don't try Because I am different **But aren't we all different?**	1) How did you feel when you read the title of this poem? 2) What does the author want students to learn from this poem? 3) How would you describe the student? 4) What should the student do? 5) Do you know anyone who feels like this student? 6) Does the poem cause you to feel empathy for the student? Describe. 7) Is the last line a profound sentence? Specify. 8) How could you help a student who feels like the student?

Poem: A Loss

Author's purpose: To show how crucial a game can be to students' ego.

New Outlook: Point out the things that the student did well during the game, such as good teamwork or individual skills. Focus on encouraging and motivating them to do better in the future.

A Loss

We come through a crowd that's high spirited
We sold a lot of tickets
<u>The crowd was looking wicket</u>
This game can be our pivot
Making me seen a litter incoherent

But we have to flow
<u>I feel like a Bro</u>
<u>I must put on a show</u>

This game must reach a new plateau
I threw the ball to my Bro

He caught the pass
But it wasn't a fast enough dash

<u>We lost the game</u>
All I saw was a flash
<u>Now I feel like trash</u>
I can't take the rehash
Or the student's backlash

We didn't win the game
But next time we will reclaim

Insightful Questions

1) Why do you think the author chose the title?

2) Describe the student's feelings.

3) How does the poem make you feel? Specify.

4) Do you think the student could have avoided his reaction?

5) What inference solutions should the student try? Describe.

6) Do you think there are students who feel like the student? Elaborate.

7) Would sharing calming strategies with the class be helpful?

8) What would you suggest to a student who faces challenges like the student?

Poem: Leave Me Alone

Author's objective: To share how students' personalities start acting like their friend and it is unacceptable.

New Outlook: Consolingly speak to the students privately. Pull them aside during a break or after class to ask about their new behavior. Ask them if everything is okay. The student may not know they are changing.

Leave Me Alone

I never thought I would ever hear

You say, "Leave me alone."

You said you do not want anyone in your zone

Son, you have changed your tone

I do not like the behavior that you have shown

Remember, you are not grown

You are making the family moan

"Child, I'm your mom!"

Without me, you would not be born

Why are you making me feel like a stone?

Do not become your friend's clone

Insightful Questions

1) Why do you think the author wrote this?

2) What is your opinion of the student's behavior? Describe

3) Should the parent understand some take longer to respond to direction? Explain.

4) How does the student respond? Specify.

5) Complete the chart. Discuss what it shows:

Self-Reflection   Student Reflection

6) Does this poem provide a good learning experience? Explain

7) What connections can you make after reading the poem? Describe

8) Should the student do a self-reflection? Specify.

9) Can the student refocus their point of view? How?

Uplifting The Pain...Growth Mindset

Poem: Shaking

Author's goal: To draw attention to students who have trembling reactions. Such an overtake is attributed to the students 'nerves or anxieties.

New Outlook: Shaking or trembling is a natural response to certain situations and does not define who you are as a student. It is important to approach students with tolerance, compassion, and understanding. Help by contributing to a calm safe and encouraging environment.

Shaking

I am shaking
It is so heartbreaking
Each morning I'm waking

My legs, my hands start shaking
This such an undertaking
Sometimes it makes me vomit
Heart racing, crying
Nervously, I just keep on trying

I'm shaking
This feeling people look with such a mistaking
They think I'm faking
They need an awakening

My nerves cause such an overtaking
Simply because I'm shaking
And my heart is aching

This is not to be taken as a joke
And doesn't deserve a poke
Some need to get woke
Before they spoke
Can't you feel me?

Insightful Questions

1) If you see a student shaking, should you laugh and point at them?

2) What can you say to a student who is shaking before they go into class?

3) What can you ask your teacher if you see a student shaking?

4) Should you help a student if they are nervously shaking?

5) If you saw someone who displayed behavior like the student, would you be understanding?

6) Have you ever experienced nervousness like the student?

7) Does this poem make you feel sensitive towards a student with similar experience?

Poem: Contrary

Author's purpose: To describe how some students are not agreeable and have a negative attitude.

New Outlook: Acknowledging other student's thoughts and feelings makes it easier to find a way to work together with students to find a solution.

Contrary

On my way to school
<u>I said what are you looking at fool?</u>
She said "You're so cruel"
I said "It's because I'm cool"
<u>"And I don't have to follow anyone's rule"</u>

I walk into class
Acting all rash
As soon as I can, I'm going to take a dash
I asked a student, "Whatcha looking at?"

He said "Nothing"
<u>I respond, "I'm not a nothing, I'm a something"</u>
I secretly take out my phone
All I heard was the dial tone

Snatched
Because the rules are well-known
Teacher said "You'll get it back before a hailstorm"

The class is taking turns reading
I sit down and look for my book
That is all it took

Suddenly, the teacher called on me
I don't know why
I holler, "You know that I can't see"
Someone snickers
I scream "Shut up before I make you beg and plea"

I have problems breaking down words to read
So, I announce to the class that "They had better take heed"

Insightful Questions

1) What does the author want you to think about? Explain.

2) As you are reading the poem, what do you visualize?

3) Fill in the chart. Compare and discuss:

What you Know   What you have learned

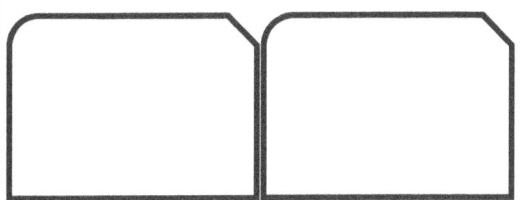

4) Why is this poem important?

5) Do you know a student whose behavior has been misunderstood because of their reaction? Describe.

6) How would you have felt if you were the student?

7) Should you be encouraging to a student who experiences this in class?

"Because I don't want anyone to think

That I'm a different breed"
Immediately, the teacher calls someone else
with speed

Poem: Hurt

Goal of the author: To illustrate how students are itching to release their silent emotions which cause them to feel side-down.

New Outlook: It is important to approach students with empathy and understanding. Avoid making assumptions or judgments about their struggles and instead listen and offer support.

Hurt

Silently, I'm feeling hurt
It makes me feel like dirt
Of course, I'm not a jerk
I don't want to wear a shirt

Teacher wants me to answer with perk
The students are looking with a smirk
My mom is wondering why I won't work
I'm just not feeling alert

Since silently I'm hurt
I want to let out a big blurt
I'm just feeling like an invert

So that I don't silently hurt

Some day
I'm going to put everyone… on high alert
That I'm going to assert myself
To become an extravert

Insightful Questions

1) Can silence be a sign of something seriously wrong?

2) What are some signs of how the student was feeling? Describe.

3) Does the author hope the poem provides a good learning experience?

4) Can you identify with the student?

5) How does the poem affect you when you read it? Explain.

6) Do you think there are students who feel like the student? Describe.

7) What would you suggest to a student who faces challenges like the student?

8) How can students show their support for classmates with similar problems?

9) Describe the students' thought pattern at the end of the poem?

Poem: Process

<u>Author's purpose:</u> To illustrate how information is taken in by the student but may sound odd and not understood.

<u>New Outlook:</u> It can be frustrating and concerning when students are unable to process information or understand concepts. Make sure to help set a positive tone in the classroom culture where students feel comfortable asking for help and making mistakes.

Process

As a child
I take in information
<u>But it sounds funny</u>
What are you saying?
What do I do?

<u>You tell me just listen</u>
<u>I am listening, but how do I process?</u>

<u>Some can take in large amounts of</u>
<u>information</u>
And some of us cannot
You tell me to just listen

As an adult
Things do not change

You direct me to turn left
At the second traffic light and
Then you change it
To turn right at the next traffic light

What did you say, what did you say?
Firmly, you tell me,

Just listen!

Enraged, I shout and blame you!
<u>Because too much too much</u>
<u>Information to process</u>
I am listening, but how do I process…

Insightful Questions

1) Have you experienced any of these scenarios?

2) Do you think the student could hear clearly?

3) Describe the student's challenge.

4) What should a student do if they do not understand what they hear?

5) Should this poem be discussed in the classroom? Specify.

6) What do you learn from this poem?

7) Do you think you could help a student experiencing that challenge?

Uplifting The Pain…Growth Mindset

Poem: Deaf

Author's objective: To give information on how students who are hard of hearing may feel awkward as a result.

New Outlook: Be patient and give them the time they need to communicate without feeling rushed. Being deaf can present unique challenges for students. Partake in creating a more inclusive and understanding environment.

Deaf

When I could hear
Everything came in nice and clear

Now I may hear sounds
That seem muffled and down

Sometime when someone says something to me
All I can say is hum
Making me seem dumb

Then they repeat
Which sound like a beat
Daily making me feel a defeat
As my hearing depletes

If someone comes close to me
I do not always hear
Until I see them

As my hearing seems to be getting impaired
I hope that I will be spared

One day I'd like to cheer
And unstop my ear
My dear
Unfortunately, it causes me some fear
Since this is something, I'll have to persevere

Insightful Questions

1) What is the author's objective?

2) If you approach a student from behind and startle them, how do you react?

3) What can you say to a student who appears not to hear what you have said in class?

4) How could you assist a student if they have difficulty explaining themselves in class?

5) How do you feel about repeating yourself to someone who did not hear what you said?

6) Did the poem help you gain a better insight into the student's problem? Explain.

7) How could you be supportive to students who have difficulties hearing?

Poem: What's Wrong with Me?

Author's purpose: To describe how some students like to be in charge and believe they are always. correct.

New Outlook: Be a part of creating a friendly setting where students may express themselves and take chances while learning. Encourage them to view mistakes as opportunities to learn and improve.

What's Wrong with Me?

I'm never wrong

I get upset easily

I argue if you say something about me

I put people in their place

I want to be on time

I got kicked out of school

I'm critical

I'm a pessimist

I like to be in control

I have the best

I don't apologize

So, what's wrong with me?

Insightful Questions

1) How could this poem help you gain a better understanding of the student's attitude?

2) What details helped you identify with the main idea?

3) Does this poem reveal the way some students feel about themselves?

4) Do you know students like the student in the poem?

5) Complete the chart and discuss. Describe the student in the boxes below.

1)	2)
3)	4)

6) Would you feel comfortable being around the student in the poem?

7) What suggestions would you make to the student and why?

8) Do you feel like the student's attitude?

9) If this poem describes you, how do you want to be perceived?

10) Do you understand the student's point of view? Elaborate.

Uplifting The Pain...Growth Mindset

Poem: Comprehend

Author's purpose: To share how students struggle to break down information into smaller parts.

New Outlook: Remind students that it's okay to ask for help when they don't understand something. Encourage them to reach out to their teachers or classmates for clarification. Urge them to study the classwork carefully and take their time.

Comprehend

I do not get it
Read it again!

I do not get it
Listen again!

I don't get it!
Can't you see?
Can't I see what?

Can't you see what you read?
Can't you see from what you hear?

Comprehend
Close your eyes and feel the words
Take the words and build a picture
In your mind or on paper

No more
I do not get it!

Inasmuch as
You can see what you read, and
You can see from what you hear
Once you have learned how to comprehend!

Insightful Questions

1) Describe the student's reactions?

2) What strong emotions are being expressed?

3) Can you identify with the student's challenge? How?

4) Complete the chart. Compare and contrast:

You   Common   Student

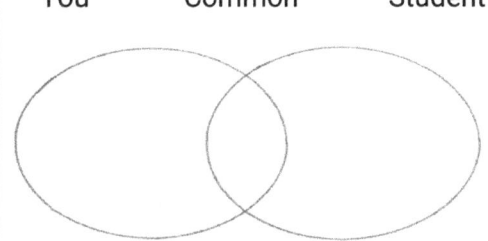

5) Do you think this is an informative poem? Specify.

6) Can you understand the student's reaction?

7) How does the poem influence your mindset and attitude towards students who experience comprehension challenges?

Poem: Wheelchair

Author's objective: To explore students daily experience with a wheelchair, highlighting their unwavering optimism despite the challenges she faces.

New Outlook: It is Important to create an inclusive and accommodating learning environment for all students. Consider becoming a buddy to help them navigate the school and classroom, as well as provide social support and friendship.

Wheelchair

Who would have thought?
Wheelchair bound
<u>It can make it difficult to get around</u>

<u>But misery I will not drown</u>
Worrying about the things that I cannot do I will not compound
Every day is like a battleground

<u>But I get up every day with a smile</u>
Because I am going to be here for a while

That's for sure
I look good so I've been told
<u>I'm going to be a Newbold</u>

I'm going to comb my hair
And look so good I declare
I make sure I smell good my dear
They look after me everywhere
Everybody just stops and cheer

Although I wish that I could stand again
That would truly be a win
But that's not possible
But I'm unstoppable

Insightful Questions

1) What does the author want you to know?

2) Do you like the student's attitude? Explain.

3) What can you learn from this poem? Specify.

4) What challenge does the student face?

5) Is it easy for the student to persevere in expressing confidence?

6) Would it be easy for you to keep following a positive mindset?

7) Can you connect with the student? Explain.

Uplifting The Pain...Growth Mindset

Poem: Not a Quarter

Author's concern: To make aware some students do not have enough money, even if it is not their fault and their parents are employed.

New Outlook: It is important to approach the situation with empathy and understanding. Extending to the student who is feeling sad because of their financial situation, let them know their feelings are valid, and you are not alone. Encourage them to reach out to friends, teachers, or other trusted adults for companionship and support.

Not a Quarter

<u>My mom doesn't have a quarter in her bag</u>
Oh, how she feels so sad
She couldn't even tell me her child, a tad

Mom went to a business meeting she had
With hope to hear something to make her glad
<u>It is embarrassing, and she feels so bad</u>

Not a quarter in her bag
Mom really hopes this is only a fad
Dag this is really a drag
<u>To be broke can make you mad</u>
Just think to be without and to be a grad
This can make anyone want to get on a launching pad…
But instead, I'll imagine I'm in Trinidad

Insightful Questions

1) What is the author's objective?

2) What is the topic of the poem?

3) What details does this poem identify to help you determine the theme?

4) How does the student express oneself?

5) Why does this poem provide a good learning experience?

6) Complete the chart. Compare and discuss:

What do you know? What you've learned? How can you help?

7) What connections can you make after reading the poem?

8) Can you sympathize with the student?

9) Have you gained a better insight into the student's problem?

10) Was the student able to refocus their point of view? How?

Poem: Get It Right

Author's purpose: To show there are students who have a difficult time handling getting an answer incorrect.

New Outlook: Remind students that making mistakes is a part of the learning process and that it is okay to get an answer wrong. Encourage them to view mistakes as opportunities to learn and improve.

Get It Right

I want to participate
So, I raise my hand
<u>I did not get it right</u>
<u>It makes me want to fight</u>
Or maybe I will try not to get uptight
I hold it in with all my might
I did not get it right

I do not want to look
Thus, get out of my sight
My temper is going to reach a height
<u>What do I do to avoid a plight?</u>
When I do not get it right

Tell me, show me
<u>I just tightly hold my fist</u>
And hope for a twist
In deep thoughts I drift
Seeking a way to shift
I tell myself
To release my fist
And not get pissed
When I do not get it right

Insightful Questions

1) Does the topic of the poem relate to you?

2) If you were the student, what steps would you take to avoid getting angry?

3) How can the student work through the challenge silently?

4) Fill in each box and discuss what it shows:

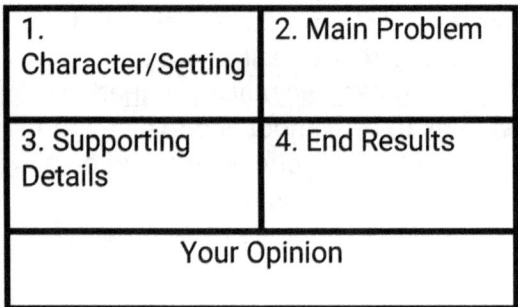

1. Character/Setting	2. Main Problem
3. Supporting Details	4. End Results
Your Opinion	

5) Could the way the students see themselves when they get an answer incorrect cause them to get angry? Explain.

6) How can you show compassion to the student?

7) How does the poem help you to gain a better insight into student dilemma?

8) Explain what happened at the end of the poem.

Poem: Smart

Author's purpose: To show how challenging it is for students to be away from peers.

New Outlook: Inclusive student engagement in enjoyable activities can help them maintain a healthy balance. If you are in a gifted class, you can use your knowledge and skills to help other students. Working together can be a great way to learn from each other and push each other to reach new heights.

Smart

I am very smart
<u>I blow spelling words off the chart</u>
Some solve math problems before most start
There are others who are great at doing art

<u>So, they pull us apart</u>
<u>It pains me to the heart</u>

I cannot help
<u>They call it gifted</u>
Should I feel uplifted?
Because our classes are shifted
I do not want to make others feel afflicted
Others make us feel depicted
Because more is predicted

It is recommended I be challenged
Because of my knowledge
It is all good but

I am still a YOUNG
Unmistakably, I just want to hang with you for a while
With others

Insightful Questions

1) What is the setting of this poem?

2) What does the poem reveal?

3) Does the student have a challenge?

4) Could this poem be true?

5) Why is this poem important?

6) How could you help this student?

7) Does this poem provide insight into gifted students' experience?

8) Is this a poem that should be discussed in class? Explain.

Poem: Looking Bleak

Author's objective: To give information on how creative students receive discouragement to complete their project.

New Outlook: Encourage students with compliments to help creative students overcome discouragement and complete their projects with confidence.

Looking Bleak

When you have or created something unique
Sometimes your path can look bleak
Making you feel so weak
It's best not to misspeak

Do I give up or
Do I continue?

Especially, when everyone around me
Tells me to give up
It's not good enough

Or they want to give a critique
Then it's like playing hide and seek
So instead, I became meek
Realizing sometimes you must tweak
So, until it's showtime, it's better to unspeak
That's natural, when its artisque

Now it's my time to speak
I'm proud because it looks like I'm on a winning streak

Insightful Questions

1) What is the message of this poem?

2) Do you think this is an inspirational poem? Specify.

3) What are some important facts to consider when you've created something new?

4) What was your favorite part? Why?

5) How could you be supportive to students who venture out and follow their dreams? Describe.

6) Did the poem help you gain a better insight into the student's challenge? Elaborate.

7) Has this poem changed your perception on trying something new? Explain.

Poem: You've Changed My World

Goal of the author: To reveal how some students have trouble understanding the role of a substitute teacher.

New Outlook: It is important to acknowledge that students may have difficulties adjusting to a substitute teacher coming into the classroom. When it occurs maintaining a positive and understanding tone and let them know that you will be there for added support.

You've Changed My World

I ask myself
Who are you?
Why are you here?
You've changed my world

What do you want?
Don't bother me
You've changed my world

I don't understand
I don't know how to feel or think
Your presence bothers me
You've changed my world

Don't come into my world because I don't trust you
I don't like change and your being here changes my environment,
My scenery, my class,
The world I'm used to
You've changed my world

Substitute Teacher Says
Now I understand because someone passes me a note
To let me know you don't like change
I'm here to help
Sorry I've changed your world

Insightful Questions

1) What is the main message of the poem?

2) Do you share the same experience?

3) How can students be prepared for transitions in the classroom?

4) Can you understand the student's attitude?

5) Was the student's reaction defiant, emotional, bad or intentional? Explain.

6) How could you encourage students who share the same challenge?

7) What is revealed in this poem?

8) How is the problem resolved?

Poem: I Don't Care

Author's purpose: To highlight a student's learning challenges, and the student expresses no concern.

New Outlook: It is important to approach them with compassion and understanding. Remind them that asking for clarification from teachers or other students is acceptable if they don't understand something. Urge them to study the information carefully and take their time.

I Don't Care	Insightful Questions
I go disappointingly, back to school again Hope I meet a friend I won't learn All I feel is a yearn	1) Is this an informative poem? Specify.
It is easier to sit there and stare 9847 divided by…	2) Is the student happy, sad, angry, or disappointed?
This math I just cannot bare I don't even care I wish my classmate would share	3) Describe an important event in the poem and tell why it is important. 4) Do you think the student should talk to a teacher about their feelings?
All this work looks like a glare I look up in the air The teacher says, "Don't you dare." I don't even care Cause I am not rare	5) Can you grasp the student's thoughts? Explain. 6) Is the problem solved by the end of the poem? Elaborate.
ALL I CAN SAY IS IT IS NOT FAIR I am just here But I won't shed a tear And I'll work on my academics next year	7) How can you cause the student to feel hopeful? Describe. 8) Does this poem improve the understanding of the student? Specify.

Poem: To Write Right

Goal of the author: To share how the students find it difficult to start and finish an essay assignment, but as they write, their concentration becomes more and more clear.

New Outlook: Encourage positive thinking among students to finish essays. Suggest seeking advice from teachers, friends, or classmates, and to keep trying despite obstacles.

To Write Right

<u>The topic might not be in sight</u>
But don't take a plight

<u>Take your pen to begin your fight</u>
As you write your focus will get ever bright
And you will finish before tonight

1 paragraph, 2 paragraphs and 3 paragraphs
Now you see the light
You can handle this bite

Now you say
My essay has taken me to a new height
Because my conclusion is so tight
So, don't ever be afraid

To Write Right

Insightful Questions

1) When you read, what pictures did you see in your mind?

2) Describe how does this poem makes you feel?

3) Why is this poem important?

4) Can you relate to the topic of this poem?

5) Is this a poem you could share with other students?

6) Can you use this poem while you attend school?

7) Exemplify how can you cause the student to feel hopeful?

8) Does the poem motivate you to write right?

Poem: Special Education

Author's purpose: To emphasize how special education is an option for those who need it.

New Outlook: Students may feel isolated or different because of their special education needs. Show them empathy and support and promote a positive and inclusive environment where everyone feels accepted and supported.

Special Education

SE can set you free

SE is where I can be me

SE is where we may have to be

SE can help people like you and me

Do math and read…don't you agree?

SE can be the place to be to succeed!

SE pride is on the rise…

This shouldn't be a surprise!

Insightful Questions

1) How do you feel after reading this poem: uncomfortable, happy, scared, or aware? Why?

2) Is this topic students are afraid to discuss? Explain.

3) Explain how do you would feel if you were receiving SE services?

4) Can this poem be helpful to students?

5) Do you think students can benefit from SE services? Elaborate.

6) If you need help, would you seek a teacher's assistance?

7) Fill in the chart. Compare and discuss:
What do you know? What you've learned. How can you help?

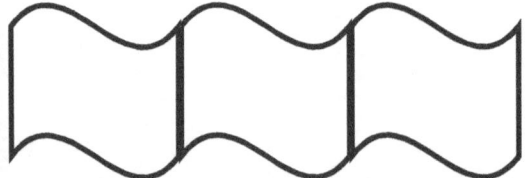

8) Did you know you can use SE services from elementary through college?

Uplifting The Pain…Growth Mindset

Poem: Take Care of Me

<u>**Author's aim:**</u> To emphasize that students are taken care of by families, schools and communities.

<u>**New Outlook:**</u> It is important to help students understand and appreciate the different people who take care of them. Share personal stories from your own life or from other students of how teachers helped students and took care of them. Stressing this includes their parents, teachers, school staff, and other caregivers.

Take Care of Me	Insightful Questions
When I was born, a doctor or midwife delivered me After I was born, the nurse in the nursery took care of me	1) What is the message of this poem?
	2) Do you think this is a valuable poem? Specify.
When I went home my mother took care of me When my mother went to work, the daycare took care of me When I go to school, my teachers taught me and took care of me	3) Is it important for a student to have a healthy relationship with a teacher?
	4) Can this poem cause you to look at adults differently, respected? Explain.
As I grow and find my way I still need people to take care of me	5) Does the poem impart insight into the world around you?
I finally get out of school to find a job And there are good days, there are bad ones, unfortunately I still may need you to take care of me	6) Can this poem be helpful to you as you grow up? Elaborate.
	7) Is it important to learn we need people? Describe.
It requires more to take care of me Please realize it takes a community or a village to take care of Me…all of us	8) After reading stanza 5 has is changed your mindset about your school community. Explain.

Poem: No Excuse

Author's wish: To let students know there are classmates that act like they don't wish to talk to other students, but they may be experiencing overwhelming loneliness.

New Outlook: It's important to avoid negative reactions such as laughing or making fun of a student's actions. Try to communicate with the person. Be patient and give them the time they need to communicate without feeling rushed.

No Excuse

<u>No excuse</u>
<u>For not acknowledging</u>

No excuse
For not being there

No excuse
For not calling

<u>No excuse</u>
<u>For not listening</u>

No excuse
For not protecting

No excuse
For not sharing

No excuse
For not taking the time

No excuse
For not being encouraging

No excuse
For not wanting to feel my pain
No excuse…

Insightful Questions

1) What does the poem remind you of?

2) Describe how the student feels.

3) Why shouldn't we judge students by what we see?

4) Who would you go to if you had those experiences?

5) Do you think the student's feelings can affect the way they treat classmates?

6) What would you say to a person who feels like the student?

7) Has the poem helped you to understand the student's sentiments?

Poem: I Didn't Mean To

Author's mission: To communicate that students have coordination challenges. They can have poor motor coordination, visual impairment, or insufficient hearing to comprehend.

New Outlook: Remember to be patient and understanding with students who have motor coordination deficit. Ensure them that you are concerned and know that with the right help they can succeed academically and socially.

I Didn't Mean To	Insightful Questions
I can walk and talk Run and jump Hear and see But sometimes they come out wrong All I can say is <u>I didn't mean to…</u> My judgement may be off, <u>Or I may not be coordinated</u> <u>Some may call it an auditory or visual</u> <u>something</u> Whatever the case All I can say is I didn't mean to… I reach for a glass of milk <u>Mistakenly, I knock it over again and again</u> I see but I cannot read clearly I walk but I may trip I listen but I cannot hear the details I may run and stumble into you… Sorry, All I can say mommy, I didn't mean to…	1) Do you think this poem is funny or serious? Specify. 2) What is the student's problem? 3) What details in the poems can help you identify the topic and the theme? 4) Does the student behavior deserve attention? 5) What are some reasons why this poem provides a good learning experience? 6) What would you have done if you were the student in the poem? 7) What suggestions do you have for the student?

Poem: I Can't Get to School

Goal of the author: To highlight how students' lives are too far away to walk to school and detest detests arriving late or missing school.

New Outlook: When a student is unable to get to school, it is important to approach the situation with empathy and understanding. Praise the students for the days they attend school. Share class work that the student may miss.

I Can't Get to School

I'm late
This is something I hate
It's too far to walk to school
I hate looking like a fool
This just isn't cool

My mom won't get up on time
It's like I go to school parttime
I try to get a ride with a friend
When I ask, they look at me like I've committed a sin

Other times I must ride the bus
All I hear is a lot of fuss
Sometimes I get to school in a car
Then I feel like a star

I can't get to school!

I hope the teachers know it's not my fault
My schoolwork is coming to a halt
My grades are starting to look like I'm in default
Sometimes I feel like my family needs a jolt
Maybe I should start a revolt

I can't get to school!

I won't give up hope
So, I'll get on a tightrope
Since I am looking forward to a future on a higher scope

Insightful Questions

1) Do you think the student should have shared their feelings with their mom?

2) What emotions is the student feeling? How do you know?

3) Does the poem deserve attention? Explain.

4) Could this poem be insightful to teachers?

5) What would you have done if you were the student?

6) How could you be supportive to the student?

7) Was the student able to change their point of origin? Describe.

Uplifting The Pain...Growth Mindset

Poem: I Got it All

Author's target: To discuss how some students do not want to receive any more material things because they have everything they want and need.

New Outlook: It is important to approach the situation with empathy and understanding. Remind the student that support can come from different sources in addition to family. Encourage them to reach out to friends, teachers, or other trusted adults for companionship and support. Let the student know that their feelings are valid, and they're not alone.

I Got It All

To some it seems I got it all, everything
Everyone sees me at the mall
I'm always standing tall
<u>If only they knew what happens at nightfall,
my sadness</u>
I have my own room
<u>Which feels like a gloom</u>
I have the latest sneakers, my Jordon's
I have surround sound speakers
I can call on my cell
And it maybe swell, to some
I have a tablet
It's just become a habit or something to do
I got money
Which causes students to become chummy?

"Honey, do you want to go to the store"
<u>"NO, because I DON'T WANT NO MORE!"</u>

To myself I think
I don't want no more
"What about some chores, mom"

Insightful Questions

1) Why do you think the author wrote this?

2) Describe how the student feels throughout the poem.

3) Have you gained a better understanding of the student's problem?

4) Fill in the chart. Compare and discuss:

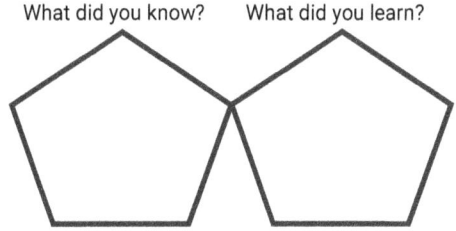

5) What would you have done if you were the student?

6) "Look at What You See," is it an important statement? Explain.

7) Has the poem caused you to discern the student's feelings? Describe.

8) How can the students' challenges be converted into a learning opportunity?

Poem: Yes, I Can

Author's objective: To encourage students to believe they may succeed if they follow their plans.

New Outlook: When the student achieves success, be sure to celebrate it with them. It is important to continue to support and encourage them while they reach their full potential.

Yes, I Can

<u>Yes, I can, if I plan</u>
Yes, I can, yes, I can
I can reach the top if I plan
Yes, I can, yes, I can

<u>I will work hard, to use my plan</u>
Yes, I can, yes, I can
I may fall, but I won't stop
I will get back to my plan
Yes, I can, yes, I can
Once I know myself, love myself and help myself,
I can work my plan
Yes, I can, yes, I can
<u>I won't stop, till I've reached my plan</u>
Because I can succeed…
Yes, I can, yes, I can, if I plan

Insightful Questions

1) How does this poem make you feel?

2) What is the message of this poem?

3) Is this a poem you could share with other students?

4) What parts of the poem are more important to you?

5) Interpret the poem in your own words.

6) Can you use any part of this poem while you attend school?

7) Has this poem changed your outlook? Explain.

Poem: Yes, I Am

Author's goal: To instill in students to be optimistic, have dignity. Be proud of who they are and to be determined to be successful.

New Outlook: Acknowledge the student's confidence in who he is and praise him for it. Serve as a source of motivation, praise their strengths and grow with him.

Yes, I am

When you see me
It doesn't mean I want to attack
So, don't overreact
Some people think I am packed

Don't think
I came from a shack
And no, I don't take no crack
As a matter of fact
I am trying to stay on track

My schoolwork
I never slack
I know how to make eye contact
So, I can effectively interact

In my opinion
VIOLENCE is whack
Don't come to me with that smack
If you don't know I have a natural knack

Just Know
POSITIVE people I will attract
I ignore all negative flack
As a result, I work hard out here so I won't lack

So, no one can call me a lazy back
Since I will counteract all
All
Just because I am well-stacked

Insightful Questions

1) What is the significance of this poem? Describe.

2) How does the student feel? Sad, happy, confident, or proud? Explain.

3) Can you identify with the poem?

4) Explain why this poem deserves attention?

5) What is your opinion of the first three lines? Describe.

6) After reading this poem, do you feel inspired to achieve your goals? Explain.

7) Do you think this is an uplifting poem? Specify.

Poem Rubric

	1	2	3	4
Author's Purpose	The student communicates and expresses author's purpose with limited effectiveness	The student communicates and expresses author's purpose with some effectiveness	The student communicates and expresses author's purpose with considerable effectiveness	The student communicates and expresses author's purpose with high degree of effectiveness
Supporting Details	The student provides supporting details (with evidence, examples, and descriptions) which are unclear, not relevant to the text, and not related to the author's purpose. Student demonstrated limited understanding of the poem.	The student provides supporting details (with evidence, examples, and descriptions) which are somewhat clear, sometimes relevant to the text, and not related to the author's purpose. Student demonstrated some understanding of the poem.	The student provides supporting details (with evidence, examples, and descriptions) which are effective, mostly relevant to the text, and not related to the author's purpose. Student demonstrated considerable understanding of the poem.	The student provides supporting details (with evidence, examples, and descriptions) which are consistently specific, relevant to text, insightful, closely related to the author's purpose. Student demonstrated limited understanding of the poem.
Conclusion	The student provides a closing sentence that is <u>very weak, unclear and does not restate</u> the topic of the poem. The student is unsuccessful in summarizing the poem.	The student provides a closing sentence that is <u>unclear and restates the topic</u> of the poem. The student is not successful in summarizing the poem.	The student provides a closing sentence that is <u>strong, clearly restates</u> the topic of the poem. The student is somewhat successful in summarizing the poem.	The student provides a closing sentence that is very strong and clearly restates the topic of the poem. The student is successful in summarizing the poem.

Mindset Building List

1. **Self-Actualization** - is the process of reaching your full potential
2. **Self-Awakening** - a recognition or coming into awareness of something
3. **Self-Awareness** - an awareness of one's own personality or individuality conscious knowledge of one's own character, feelings, motives, and desires.
4. **Self-Confidence** - is the belief in your abilities and qualities
5. **Self-Control** - is the ability to regulate your emotions, thoughts, and behaviors
6. **Self-Discovery** - the act or process of achieving self-knowledge the process of acquiring insight into one's own character.
7. **Self-Discipline** - is the ability to do what is necessary
8. **Self-Evaluation** - the ability to take a step back and figure out why something worked or didn't work was important
9. **Self-Examination** - the study of one's own behavior and motivations. A study of one's own thoughts and feelings
10. **Self-Exploration** - the practice of examining your own thoughts, feelings, values, beliefs, identity, background, views, and emotions, with the purpose of better understanding yourself
11. **Self-Observation** - serving your thoughts, feelings, and body without judgment.
12. **Self-Perception** - the view we have about ourselves, our characteristics, and the judgements we make about the traits we have
13. **Self-Reflection** - examination of one's own thoughts and feelings serious thought about one's character, actions, and motives.
14. **Self-Transcendence** - is the process of looking beyond oneself and finding meaning in helping others

Character Trait List

1. **Adaptability** - to remain content in dynamic situations
2. **Compassion** - giving value to all aspects of life
3. **Caring** - means showing kindness, love, and consideration to others
4. **Empathy** - understanding other people's emotions
5. **Fairness** - means treating everyone in a just and equal way,
6. **Impartial** - Being fair also means including everyone, no matter their differences
7. **Forgiving** - to cease to feel resentment against
8. **Generosity** - showing a readiness to give more of something,
9. **Gratitude** - the quality of being thankful; readiness to show appreciation for and to return kindness
10. **Honesty** - adherence to the facts
11. **Humble** - low estimate of one's own importance
12. **Integrity** - Knowing the importance of giving your word
13. **Kindness** - the quality of being friendly, generous, and considerate
14. **Patience** - the capacity to accept or tolerate ability to wait
15. **Respect** - being sensitive and appreciative of those around them
16. **Responsibility** - means taking ownership of your actions
17. **Reliable** - friend means you're there to help and support your friends
18. **Sympathy** - feelings of pity and sorrow for someone else's misfortune
19. **Trustworthiness** - means keeping your promises and being someone others can count on

Things to Remember

"Look at What You See"

"Listen to What You Hear"

"If You Don't Know That Your Something

"Then Nothing Can Make You Something"

Expression: Communication: verbal, behavior, feelings, physically and emotionally.

Style: A distinctive way of expressing yourself verbally, physically, feelings, emotionally and behavior

Online Resources and References

Milestone Checklist (cdc.gov)
Mental Health Disorders Center: Types, Symptoms, Treatments, Tests, and Causes (webmd.com)
Anxiety and Depression in Children | CDC
Anxiety and High Blood Pressure (calmclinic.com)
What Is Social Anxiety Disorder or Social Phobia? (webmd.com)
Panic Attack Symptoms: Shortness of Breath, Racing Heart, "https://www.webmd.com/anxiety-panic/guide/panic-attack-symptoms"&
"https://www.webmd.com/anxiety-panic/guide/panic-attack-symptoms" More (webmd.com)
Insecurity: Types, Symptoms, and How to Handle It (webmd.com)
Emotional or behavioral disability - Wikipedia
Bipolar disorder - Symptoms and causes - Mayo Clinic
Low Self-Esteem: What Are the Signs to Look "https://www.webmd.com/mental-health/signs-low-self-esteem"For "https://www.webmd.com/mental-health/signs-low-self-esteem" and How to Deal with It (webmd.com)
Oppositional defiant disorder (ODD) - Symptoms and causes - Mayo Clinic
https://www.justanswer.com/adhd -Children
ADHD in Adults - HelpGuide.org
NIMH » "https://www.nimh.nih.gov/health/topics/obsessive-compulsive-disorder-ocd"Obsessive-Compulsive Disorder "https://www.nimh.nih.gov/health/topics/obsessive-compulsive-disorder-ocd" (nih.gov)
Obsessive Compulsive Personality Disorder (OCPD) (healthline.com)
What Is Intellectual Disability? (psychiatry.org)
Developmental Delay: Symptoms, Causes, Treatment "https://www.healthline.com/health/developmental-delay"&
"https://www.healthline.com/health/developmental-delay" More (healthline.com)
Autism spectrum disorder - Symptoms and causes - Mayo Clinic
Adopted Child Syndrome - Causes, Effects "https://www.momjunction.com/articles/adopted-child-syndrome_00375730/"And "https://www.momjunction.com/articles/adopted-child-syndrome_00375730/" Ways To Prevent It (momjunction.com)C:\Users\Administrator\Downloads\Adopted Child Syndrome - Causes, Effects "https:\www.momjunction.com\articles\adopted-child-syndrome_00375730\"And NK "https:\www.momjunction.com\articles\adopted-child-syndrome_00375730\" Ways To Prevent It (momjunction.com)
Understanding Sensory Processing Disorder | Understood - For learning and thinking differences
7 Ways to Help Kids Sensitive to Hair Brushing! Your Kid's Table (yourkidstable.com)
Hair: Sensory Issues with Washing, Cutting and Brushing (thesensoryseeker.com)
24 Signs of a Highly Sensitive Person | Psychology Today
Dyslexia Symptoms in Children and Adults by Age, Risk Factors, How to Diagnose (webmd.com)
What Is Dyscalculia | Understood - For learning and thinking differences
What is Dysgraphia? Disorder of Written Expression Signs and Symptoms (additudemag.com)
Dyspraxia - symptoms, "https://www.healthdirect.gov.au/dyspraxia"treatments "https://www.healthdirect.gov.au/dyspraxia" and causes |"https://www.healthdirect.gov.au/dyspraxia"healthdirect
Dysarthria (Slurred Speech): Symptoms, Types, Causes, Treatment (webmd.com)
Apraxia of speech - symptoms, "https://www.healthdirect.gov.au/apraxia-of-speech"diagnosis "https://www.healthdirect.gov.au/apraxia-of-speech" and treatment | health direct
https://www.parentingspecialneeds.org/article/dysnomia
https://meadowscenter.org/wp-content/uploads/2022/04/TurnAndTalk_TeacherGuide1.pdf
https://ucincinnatipress.pressbooks.pub/oralcommunication/chapter/__unknown__-6/
https://www.examples.com/english/miscommunication-between-teacher-and-students.html#google_vignette
https://floridarti.usf.edu/resources/gtips/GTIPS_3rdEd.pdf
https://advancingstudentsforward.org/
https://positivepsychology.com/empathy-worksheets/
https://theimagineproject.org/wp-content/uploads/2020/07/The-Imagine-Project-Elementary-Lessons.pdf
https://characterstrong.com/purposefull-people/
https://www.medinah11.org/Downloads/SEL%20CURRICULUM%20HANDBOOK%20-%20Nov%202015%20for%20printing.pdf
https://www.reedschools.org/cms/libCA1001640/Centricity/Domain/462/Sixth%20Grade%Social-Emotional%20Guidebok.pdf
https://soeonlne.american.edu/blog/growth-mindset-in-the-classroom/
http://thehub.polk-fl.net/pd/wp-content/uploads/sites/13/Teacher-and-Administrator-SAO-Manual-revisions-for-21-22-Final.pdf
https://www.bell-foundation.org.uk/eal-programme/guidance/classroom-guidance/great-ideas/collaborative-activities/
https://advancingstudentsforward.org/
https://www.merriam-webster.com/dictionary
https://copilot.microsoft.com/
https://www.google.com/search?
https://www.splashlearn.com/blog/character-traits-for-kids/
https://www.partnerwithschools.org/character-education.html?
https://www.linkedin.com/pulse/7-character-traits-master-personal-professional-business-paulie-scott/

Who is the Author

Gail Carter-Cade is a mother, educator, entrepreneur, and writer who experienced, firsthand, the challenges families face when trying to understand the emotional and mental struggles of another family member and the manifestations of those struggling in their behavior and learning styles. She attended college in New York and majored in Business Administration with a minor in Journalism. Upon realizing that she could serve a greater need through her passion for helping and educating others, she went back to college and changed her major to education. She has volunteered and worked at elementary and middle schools in Jacksonville, Florida, supporting students with a variety of abilities, behavior patterns, learning styles, and personalities.

This book of poems reflects her innate ability to connect with and understand how different behavioral and learning styles are. Her poetry brings transparency to the drivers of people's behavioral and learning styles and opens the doors for deeper discussions.

Are you, like so many people, puzzled because you cannot quite describe, understand, or explain what you have seen or experienced:
- You continuously have traumatic thoughts or memories that seem real to this day.
- An employee cannot explain why they are struggling and not making progress.
- A student is constantly in trouble in school.

For these deeply troubling scenarios, it has been hard to admit, disclose and "let out" the underlying pain-until now.

This resourceful poetry book was inspired by the writer's personal experience of uplifting this pain in her daughters and her family. It will show how behaviors and learning styles can manifest themselves in our lives. This extraordinary book is easy to read and provides relatable, poetic imagery of real-life experiences that may invoke insightful "aha" moments. It will be useful at home, in a classroom, or in a workplace setting.

No more grasping for words for an explanation. No more agony from not knowing or understanding what you have witnessed or felt. Now you can uplift the pain and embrace others and your behavioral and learning styles through these informative transparent poems. Gail Carter-Cade is available for encouraging, training, speaking and consulting.
Contact gailcarter-cade@upliftingthepain.com
The website www.upliftingthepain.com will be available as a resource for parents, students, educators, employers and new book releases.